GREAT WESTERN AS

Imagery and Information

Compiled by Kevin Robertson

ISBN 978-1-909328-30-3

First published in 2015 by Crécy Publishing Ltd. under the Noodle Books imprint

Crécy Publishing Ltd. Unit 1a Ringway Trading Estate, MANCHESTER M22 5LH

www.crecy.co.uk

Printed in Turkey and managed by Jellyfish Solutions

Front cover - The archetypal Great Western branch line terminus, this one is Wallingford prior to closure in 1959. There could hardly be said to be a standard design for the station at the end of a branch line, most having come about in consequence of the absorption into the system of an originally independent concern and which then came with a variety of design features. Where these were considered adequate they were retained although if facilities were limited (Lambourn) or were deemed necessary to be replaced (Abingdon) then 'standard' designs contemporary with the period were provided. Regardless of the location there were invariably some prerequisite requirements: passenger facilities, goods facilities, and usually engine servicing facilities. Each location might also draw upon the one local type of traffic (at Wallingford it was a maltings) which would be a welcome boost to the revenue for the branch. (Tourism, milk, cattle, racehorses are other examples - the list is probably endless.) Seen here the auto-train waits at Wallingford ready for its journey back to the main line at Cholsey. Regretfully despite the warm sunshine of a spring / summers day, decline is all too evident. Faded paintwork and a none too clean locomotive are indicative of a railway where revenue was now seriously compromised. Some economy has already taken place with the removal of the siding leading to the locomotive shed and it will not be long before passenger services cease. The aspirations of the promoters almost a century before in 1861 to link with the Watlington branch at the latter's Oxfordshire terminus have been banished. Fortunately the railway would survive for general goods traffic until 1965 by which time a new maltings plant had also been established near the railway. This would ensure its survival for goods until 1981. Meanwhile the Great Western Society made several forays with their own auto-train over the branch on enthusiasts' outings - British Rail would also use the branch for static photography of their new High-Speed train sets. All this came to an end after traffic to and from the maltings finally ceased in 1981. It was at this point that the Cholsey & Wallingford railway society was formed to preserve the line. Unfortunately what was not saved was the actual terminus at Wallingford although it is now once more possible to travel from a new station close to the site of the original along the route of the branch back to a separate platform at Cholsey on the main line.

Title page - Ten miles north-east of Wallingford was the intended destination of the route at Watlington. History would determine the proposed railway would never proceed beyond Wallingford so leaving Watlington to be served by a branch from Princes Risborough. This undated 1950s view depicts the arrival of a train at the Oxfordshire terminus, a time when cycles were welcome. Little will have changed from previous decades, the railway providing a service to the community when there was little alternative transport - it should be said of course that rural communities were also far less mobile. Times though they were a 'changing', considering the number of passengers 2-3, and the number of railway staff 3-4. It cannot be said that with such figures this was in any way a profitable working under BR, especially against a tide of ever increasing operating costs whilst revenue remained either stubbornly set to that of times past or was even decreasing. It would not be long before the accountants at Paddington would realise the futility of services, passenger trains ceasing at the end of June 1957. We may perhaps wonder what the ladder was doing propped against the bunker of the pannier tank?

Rear cover - Old locomotive boilers in use as a stationary steam supply - possibly at Wolverhampton but this is not confirmed. (Normally only one boiler would be provided so to have two this would be the hallmark of a major depot.) The boilers would likely have been installed when the shed was built and provided a steam supply for cleaning boiler tubes etc. Usually the most junior fireman available would be tasked with firing, which when steam was required in volume could almost be as demanding as anything he would likely face on a later main-line career. Notice the difference in design of the smokebox, the older type being on the left replete with its riveted ring and bezel to the door.

-

CONTENTS

Note - Reference to the geographical areas for the various GWR 'Divisions' are as close as possible to Traffic Department boundaries. It should be mentioned variations existed when comparing the boundaries of the Traffic Divisions with those of the Engineering Department Divisions.

INTRODUCTION

This is a book I have wanted to compile for some time. Notwithstanding Noodle Books perhaps more well-known proliferation with Southern based titles ('The Southern Way' series in particular), I will admit to a lasting fondness of the Great Western. The result has been the squirreling away of odd snippets of information as well as photographs which I hoped one day to use in a 'miscellany' type volume.

Now that opportunity presents itself and at last I can show to a wider audience some of the odd items that have been cluttering up drawers and files for some time.

Please do not expect a full history of the GWR, that has been done by others far more qualified than the present writer and covering most aspects. Instead this is a collection of pieces perhaps slightly off beat but I also hope of interest. Most that has been chosen is also deliberately unpublished.

Neither does it follow a theme, instead the idea was to include what I have personally found of interest - and I sincerely hope you will too.

One area I have a particular fascination with for some years has been the 'Economic System of Maintenance', better known perhaps as the 'Occupation Key' system. Unfortunately to use the latter phrase is not to do justice to what was at the time a revolution in maintaining a length of railway with fewer men and as time passed with what was then the height of technology. It was a system that was so successful it was developed on literally hundreds of miles of railway and subsequently copied by both the LNER and the Southern. However, notwithstanding my own fascination with this aspect of history I have had to recognise that not all will share my enthusiasm, hence what is reproduced is but part of an 80,000 word text. Today there is not a single system of line, public or private that retains this feature although some aspects of the type of equipment remain in use for other purposes.

There could also be more on the GW in the future, so as mentioned on the final page, do please let me or the publisher know if this type of approach appeals. There is still at least one drawer full waiting!

Kevin Robertson
Corhampton 2015

Finding new images of broad-gauge days is rare these days, but here is one that hopefully has not had a wide circulation in the past. Newton Abbot in May 1892, the original print stating, "Train of Broad Gauge engines prior to leaving for Swindon."

The end of the Broad Gauge

Notwithstanding Brunel's support for the Broad Gauge and regardless whether there was actual advantage in having rails 7'0¼" apart, it was always going to be a question of sheer weight of numbers as to whether broad or standard gauge would prevail.

The situation which had arisen at Gloucester involving the tran-shipment of goods is well known and had indeed been the subject of more than one cartoon in the popular press of the time. Less well known is that similar difficulties had occurred in other locations, Yeovil, Exeter and Salisbury to name but three whilst in South Wales, such was the growing antipathy towards what was seen by many as a growing case of isolationism that some 296 companies sent petitions to the GWR Board in favour of converting to the narrow gauge track. It was ironic that some of these were the very same companies who years before, had been jubilant upon the arrival of the first (broad gauge) railway.

It was then only a matter of time before arguments for the conversion began to win the day. Despite Gooch's sense of loyalty towards his mentor I K Brunel, he, as chairman of the board, reluctantly supported some of the essential changes, particularly where the effect would be felt most by the company, and that was in its massive revenue earning coal trade.

With the decision made, events began to improve and by 1869 things began to turn in favour of the GWR. At the March Board meeting, Gooch stated, "Everywhere but in the West of England the broad gauge rails are being taken up, and the rolling stock is being converted to narrow gauge as quickly as possible, the 'corner' has been turned at last, and there is every prospect of a prosperous future."

The Broad Gauge lines he was referring to were those between Gloucester and Hereford and which connected the GWR to the narrow gauge line to Shrewsbury providing a narrow gauge link to the north of England. The Hereford line, connecting as it did to the lines of the South Wales Railway would enable the GWR to tap the lucrative coalfields and so run trains to the north of England without a break of gauge.

The line between Hereford and Grange Court, a distance of 22 miles, was converted to narrow gauge over five days in August 1869. During its closure for conversion, passengers were conveyed between stations by ten first class stage coaches hired from a local omnibus company. (Could

In 1874 it was found that the standard method then being used for narrowing the gauge by moving the outside longitudinal rail into its narrow gauge position, meant that it was moved on to ground that had not been compacted by engines running over it. This would eventually upset the balance of the track through the rail sinking into the softer earth. It was after an inspection by the Board of Trade who had declared some lines to be dangerous as a result, that the company at their August 1874 meeting decided to take this opportunity to substitute its longitudinal lines with cross-sleeper track using steel rails in place of iron and to use the heavier 801b instead of 681b rails.

Cornwall Railway train at Saltash c1870. In the background Brunel's famous bridge over the Tamar was then just 11 years old.

Because of the company's heavy coal traffic, the first 60 miles of road to be relaid was on the South Wales lines where this type of traffic was about to increase considerably. This programme continued for over 20 years, adding millions in revenue to the company's capital programme. At their meeting of August 1894, the Chief Engineer Mr. Inglis recommended the directors to increase the pace of the track relaying schedule. This was agreed with more funds being allocated to the cross sleeper programme in the anticipation that it would take another two or three years before completion.

this be the first incident of a road-replacement bus service?)

To complete this prodigious undertaking, the GWR used 450 of its permanent way staff brought in from the Northern and Aberdare Districts, plus others from all points as far away as Milford Haven. Working a 20-hour day didn't allow much time for sleeping, but accommodation was provided by a forty-vehicle broad gauge 'sleeping train', consisting of covered wagons that had been carefully whitewashed and supplied with an abundance of clean straw and new sacks for the men to lie on. The conditions of the exercise meant that the men worked and slept without a change of clothes until all 22 miles had been completed. Fortunately the weather was kind in that second week of August; had it been the reverse not even the sturdiest wagon would have kept the straw dry and inviting for the men.

In addition to the sleeping wagons a supplies van formed part of the staff train. It carried amongst its equipment braziers on which the men cooked their food. Each man brought his own supply of food for the week for which he received a daily allowance of just over one shilling.

Even though the line had been laid down as broad gauge track in 1853, it did not become GWR owned until many years after, therefore sleepers were used in its construction, the heavy duty rail bolted to the sleepers using 3,800 bolts per mile. During the narrowing these bolts were unscrewed from the sleepers, the rail was moved 28 inches sideways and after new holes had been augured through the sleepers, it was bolted back in place using hand spanners to draw up the nuts from beneath the sleepers.

An operation of this size would undoubtedly have an adverse affect on trade. Thus there were months of initial planning to minimise any losses. The work was carried out by the company's Chief Engineer William George Owen, who had succeeded to the post after the death of Brunel, his main assistants on the project were J. Ward Armstrong: Divisional Engineer, Hereford division and W. Lancaster Owe:, District Engineer, Gloucester.

The next major operation was the narrowing of the gauge between Oxford and Maidenhead and the removal of the third line from the mixed gauge between Oxford and Wolverhampton, which apparently had never carried broad gauge stock over its rails. The extent of these operations made it essential that the large amount of permanent way stores required could be delivered on site when needed. This function was not at this time under the control of Swindon, but was ordered from the engineering stores at Paddington.

All this time criticism at the company meetings and in the contemporary press of the broad gauge was rife, the 'Railways News' in its August 1869 edition asked, "How greatly improved would have been the position of this property (the GWR) if these changes had never been rendered necessary and the battle of the gauges had never been fought."

At the February shareholders meeting in 1871, Sir Daniel Gooch raised the Broad Gauge question again when he referred to it as a matter of the greatest importance, "... and recommend the alteration of the gauge, once and for all". Thus it was that he had finally come to accept that the principles for which he had once stood shoulder to shoulder with Brunel to protect and which had also once been hailed as a significant engineering achievement had turned out to

The old Goods Shed and Blacksmith's shop at Newton Abbot and what certainly appears to be an incident of sorts.

be a millstone around the neck of the GWR. As if to confirm this decision, a further report in the 'Railway News' on 4 March 1871, read, "The conversion of the broad into narrow gauge has become an absolute necessity for the Great Western. Of course it is to be regretted that the broad or exceptional gauge was ever introduced, but the only course now left open to repair the mistake is to retrace the steps erroneously taken as quickly as possible."

The GWR board at their March meeting of that year agreed to convert the broad gauge in South Wales to narrow gauge and raised £l million to finance it.

Just over a year later at the August 1872 shareholders' meeting, Gooch reported that with reference to the gauge change, the company had converted 500 miles of single line in the space of four weeks without a single accident.

The resulting net increase in trade for the next six months amounted to £169,258 and witnessed the return of good fortune for the company, but it had cost £225,000 for narrowing the line and a further £180,000 for rolling stock conversion. The GWR had developed a highly efficient method of converting the line, which was mounted in a military style campaign for speed and safety with the minimum loss of traffic, although many private firms with broad gauge sidings did not agree with the last sentiment and were to lose considerable amounts of trade while their sidings and rolling stock were being replaced.

In the first part of the operation, broad gauge stock would be gradually reduced off the line, then several weeks before the conversion, gangs of men would remove the ballast so that the wood and iron work was exposed and the transoms partially sawn through. At the time of the actual conversion these transoms would be fully severed and the timber baulk complete with rail moved into its new position and made secure.

Where the rails were laid on chairs and sleepers, additional chairs would be laid, so that the rails were simply moved from the old to the new chairs. As soon as possession of the line had been handed over to the Engineer, thousands of men would spread along the length of track and work in small gangs for up to 18 hours a day sleeping at night in horse-boxes, coaches and sheds which had been provided as accommodation for the gangs, and brought to the site by staff trains.

The work referred to by Daniel Gooch was carried out in two halves, first the narrowing of the gauge between Milford Haven and Gloucester being completed in just two weeks followed by the section between Gloucester and Swindon. This marked the completion of the change from broad to narrow gauge between Swindon and Milford Haven via Gloucester, at that time the only direct route from Swindon to South Wales as the Severn Tunnel was yet to be dug. This left the company with mixed gauge from Swindon to Paddington, and broad gauge only from Swindon to Bristol and on to the West.

While these changes made life easier for journeys between Gloucester and Birmingham, it had in fact transferred the chaos and inconvenience of the break of gauge to Swindon. The result meant that passengers and freight arriving at Swindon from Gloucester on the narrow gauge and wanting to continue west, were compelled to change and be transhipped on to the broad gauge. To accomplish this, the company built a new goods shed where freight could be transferred from narrow to broad gauge wagons, leaving passengers to pick up their broad gauge train at the railway station.

Some members of the travelling public had also become fed-up with the lineside clutter of derelict broad gauge wagons and in 1874 a complaint was made to Daniel Gooch about the enormous accumulation of trucks that for a long time had been standing on the line between Hungerford and Reading and extending over several miles. Gooch replied that these wagons had been taken off the South Wales lines and were due to undergo conversion. In addition with the narrowing of the gauge in South Wales gathering momentum, it was not possible to stable all of the broad gauge stock waiting for conversion or scrap at Swindon, thus temporary sites had to be found anywhere on the system where empty track could used.

The first narrow gauge train ran on the South Wales section of the GWR on Sunday 12 May 1872. After this the narrowing of the gauge gathered pace for a short while and in 1874 the 200 miles of line on the southern district, Chippenham to Weymouth and the Berks and Hants line, was converted to narrow gauge in two days.

Seventy broad gauge engines were taken off the Weymouth line and had to be replaced by newly built

As an example of the materials required, a Stores committee meeting of 12 February 1890 involving the Chief Storekeeper, accepted the recommendation by Mr Dean that tenders should be invited for the supply of Carriage Timber, while the Directors accepted tenders for the supply of 3,000 'Clean Broad Gauge Sleepers' measuring 10'0" x 10" x 5" at 3/9d each from the firm of Messrs. Hurt, Boulton & Haywood to be delivered to the Hayes Creosoting Works of the GWR. Also for 20,000 'Creosoted Broad Gauge Sleepers' 11'0" x 10" x 5" at 5/6d each from Messrs. R & R Bayly to be delivered at Plymouth Station.

Also mentioned is the firm of Messrs Alexanders & Co., who agreed to supply 194 loads of clean 'Quebec Yellow Pine longitudinals' 14" x 7" at 110/- shillings per load delivered to Hayes. The committee agreed to the contract but only if the firm would accept a price of 105/- shillings per load. (The outcome is not reported.)

At the same committee meeting 100 tons of scrap steel tyres were sold at £4 per ton and 10 tons of scrap gun metal axle boxes at £50 per ton.

4-2-2 'Crimea', one of 25 members of the 'Alma' class built at Swindon in October 1878. The engines of this class which were identified by name and not number, were built between June 1870 and as late as August 1888. All but two lasted until the end of the broad gauge although the first built, 'Estaffete' had been withdrawn for almost four years before the last two were in service. The position of the communication bell and also the re-railing jack may be noticed. The location is not given.

On the 21 June 1890, members of the Directors Stores Committee made a visit to Swindon Works and were met by William Dean, Loco and Carriage Superintendent who conducted them on a tour of the Works. They had travelled to Swindon in one of Mr Dean's convertible coaches especially designed so as to be able to be switched from broad to narrow gauge in readiness for the final gauge conversion which was to take place two years later. On the run down from London the coach was in the broad gauge mode and while at Swindon the Directors watched its conversion to narrow gauge in the Carriage Workshops by lifting its body from its broad gauge bogies and replacing these with a narrow gauge set ready for their return journey to Paddington. It is reported that the conversion took only ten minutes to complete: this was also stated to be a special demonstration. Even so the normal time taken for a similar conversion was said to be just 20 minutes.

narrow gauge stock. The upshot of this frenzied activity was a huge expansion in the size of Swindon Works whilst to quote from contemporary reports once again, "...the works now stretched a distance of one and three quarters of a mile in one direction by half a mile in the other."

The Broad Gauge system was destined to last another 22 years, but Sir Daniel Gooch was not to live to witness it for he died at his home, Clewer Park, near Windsor, in October 1889. It was not until the 22 May 1892 that the Broad Gauge ceased to exist with the conversion of the remaining Broad Gauge line in the West from Exeter to Penzance.

Once again a massive amount of work found its way to Swindon with the demand for new narrow gauge vehicles although this time around, much of it had been prepared in advance and constructed as convertible stock which only

needed to have narrow gauge bogies fitted in place of the broad gauge type, plus the step boards altered on the carriages. Apart from a few hundred wagons sent to the Wagon Works at Bridgwater, all of the rolling stock came to Swindon either for demolition or to be replaced. Of the 195 broad gauge Locomotives received in the Works 130 were convertible, the remainder being scrapped. Meanwhile on the passenger side, 748 coaches needed to be replaced or converted while 3,400 wagons or vans were replaced in the same way. To cater for this sudden influx of rolling stock, thirteen miles of sidings had to be laid for its reception.

Throughout its 55 years existence, the broad gauge had attracted a great deal of criticism, mainly because of the problem of transferring goods on to the narrow gauge. A further report in the "Railway News" seemed to gloat over its demise, "The 7ft gauge failed to establish its just claim asserted by Brunel for speed and steadiness in motion, in fact he is reported to have stated to the Gauge Commission, that perfection in railway travelling could not be obtained until the gauge was 14 feet wide".

This article is an abridged extract from his unpublished manuscript 'Off the Shelf', the history of the GW and BR(W) stores departments 1835 - 1995 by J S Hayward. A copy of the text is deposited in the library of 'STEAM' at Swindon. Accompanying illustrations courtesy Great Western Trust.

Above *- C B Collett (in bowler hat) with other dignitaries and VIPs admiring 'Tiny' on Newton Abbot station. 'Tiny' had been built for the South Devon railway in 1868 and operated until 1883. It then served as a stationary engine in the pump house at Newton Abbot before being placed on display at the rebuilt Newton Abbot station.*

Below *- 'Tiny' in its resting place for 44 years: the pump house at Newton Abbot.*

Left and bottom *- Stages in the cutting of the eastern end of Alderton tunnel between Hullavington and Badminton. Because of the length of cutting required to be excavated at either end, two vertical shafts were sunk from the hill-top, 280yds apart and a maximum of 140yds from the end. Digging then took place from the centre headings. Progress was estimated at 24 yards per month, the length of the completed bore intended to have been 506 yards although official records also indicate 528yds. On the basis of the progress reported, construction would have occupied 22 months. Coinciding with the construction, an influx of navvy was reported both in nearby Alderton village and at a special navvy camp set up near the western end of the tunnel.*

All the views in this section are courtesy of David Foster-Smith

The New Railway

The railway from Wootton Bassett to Stoke Gifford may be said to have been the last major new line built by the GWR. True still to come were the various cut-offs, but these could never be compared in scale with the near 30 miles of new railway through virgin territory encompassing also seven new stations.

A history of the construction has been told before (see 'GWR The Badminton Line: a portrait of a railway' by Kevin Robertson and David Abbott., Alan Sutton Publishing 1988), and in which a set of constructional views from the contractor, S Pearson & Son, was included.

Some years later in 2010 a chance conversation with David Foster-Smith on a totally unconnected topic, revealed that one of Mr Foster-Smith's forbearers had been a navvy missionary on, of all places, the construction of the new line.

David Smith (b1866), had earlier been involved in the moral and spiritual welfare of workers engaged in building the Meon Valley line in Hampshire, in the course of which he took a series of images showing the railway in stages of construction.

At the same time he appears to have been involved in a similar role for the men working on the Badminton line project, especially it appears in the area of Chipping Sodbury. It would appear likely that he divided his time between both projects. It was pure chance that in viewing the Meon Valley views (most are little more than tiny snapshots pasted in a series of albums) that this new set of views was discovered. It is a privilege to present a small selection as a record of railway building now over a century ago.

Above *- The eastern end of Alderton tunnel. Excavation of the approach cutting is almost complete and it would appear work on the tunnel also progresses. Notice the crude crossover immediately behind the 'steam navvy'. Wagons would be pushed up on the left hand line one at a time, filled with spoil, and then hauled away. The men are taking a break in their labours to observe the photographer. Notice too that ladder! A train of wagons is also present on a temporary track on the right hand side top of the cutting - possibly these would contain bricks ready to be lowered down for lining the tunnel. . At the top may also be seen a ventilation chimney and derrick.*

Unfortunately there is no index or list of dates accompanying the images although that above does state "Old Sodbury Mission and Missioner's hut". This was a time in history when the family of an itinerant worker would accompany him from one contract to another, accommodation being provided for families in separate huts or dormitories for single men

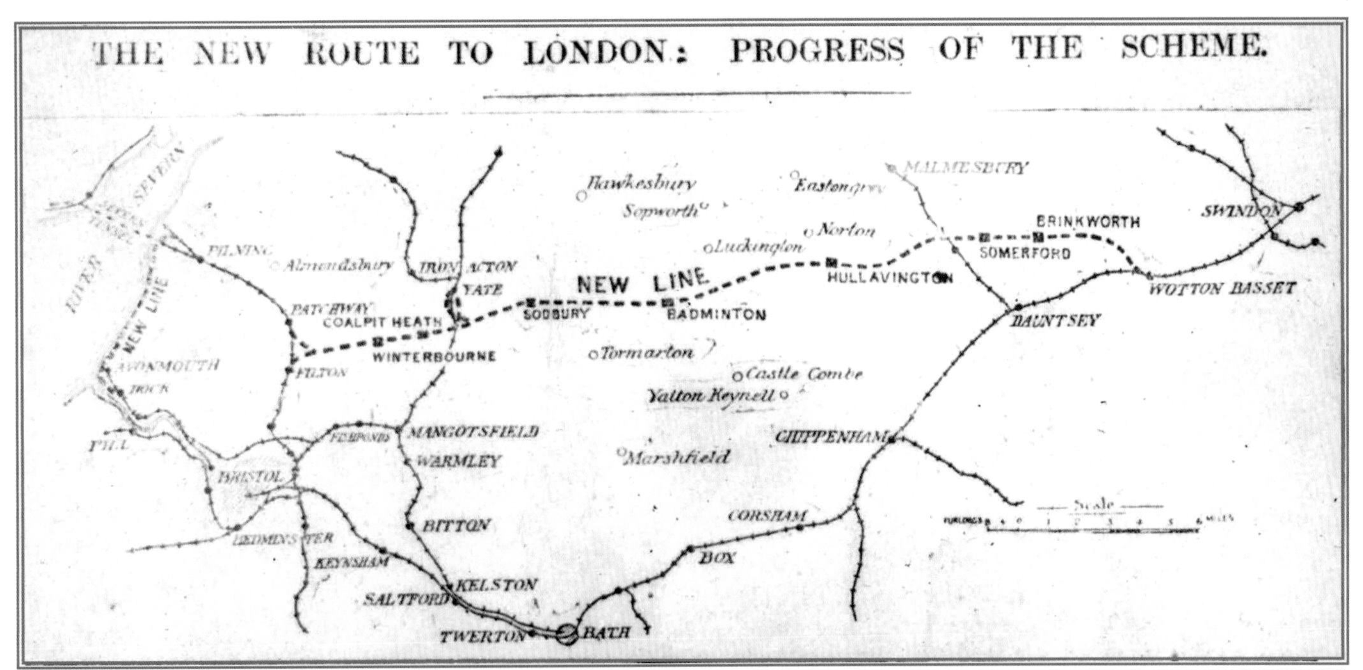

***Opposite bottom -** Navvy encampment at Lye Grove, Sodbury with (in the background) excavated material from a tunnel shaft and, running from it past the back of the huts, one of the temporary access railways. The outside 'privvys' will be noted as will the chickens and women gathered around the rear of the first hut. It is likely that the huts were shared by more than one family. In the distance on the road could well be a tradesman making a delivery, the facilities semi-permanent in nature as construction of the two-mile tunnel was easily the greatest feat of engineering.*

***Above -** Dumb-buffered wagons on temporary track. The rudimentary hand-brakes will be noted. The cutting sides have drainage channels provided whilst above is what is likely to be huts used as accommodation by the navvys.*

(Chipping) Sodbury tunnel (sic), showing, ***opposite****, the interior looking towards one of the exits and with some Victorian fingerprints remaining on the original print. It was reported that 2,500 men were employed in the making of the tunnel, not just underground of course but also men (and boys) engaged at the various shaftheads.*

This page *- The western end of the tunnel at various stages in construction. In the lower view a temporary access track may be seen. There were several of these at various locations along the route, often laid across fields with little regard for gradients. They were used to ferry materials and spoil to and from the sites of works.*

Top *- Sodbury tunnel west end with smoke rising from one of the engines at the top of what would later be a ventilation shaft. At least one steam driven air pump was needed to assist in the building. The trackwork is clearly still that provided by the contractor.*

Left *- Sodbury tunnel 'Nippers League', one of several groups of young navvys. David Smith is posed with the boys, leaning against the fence on the right. (David had a family of his own and presumably lived in nearby accommodation.) In the background the notice board gives times of weekday evening activities - which the boys and men were encouraged to attend, the idea being to keep them occupied out of work hours and away from other temptations.*

The line of Sodbury tunnel took the railway under land owned by the Duke of Beaufort. Seven vertical shafts, each 12' in diameter, were sunk at varying intervals along the course of the tunnel and from which digging was undertaken. Later, when the cuttings leading to the ends of the tunnel had been completed, it was also possible to dig inwards from the ends. The deepest of the vertical shafts was 279'. It was down these shafts that men would be lowered via a winding engine placed at the top. A temporary line of rails was provided to transport materials to each shaft. From deep below excavated materials would be brought to the surface and used to form a mound. When work was complete, six of the shafts were retained for ventilation, a castellated tower was built around the top of each shaft. This design was determined so as not to spoil the view from the Duke's ancestral home at Badminton House. The towers were granted Grade 2 listing in July 2012.

Top - *A winding engine, temporary railway, mound and ventilation tower in place. There was also an air-pump. The existence of these vents has in recent years allowed for high speeds to be maintained through the tunnel without experiencing the unpleasant effect of pressure-waves from passing trains.*

Right - *Reported as 'Old Sodbury tunnel, contractors engineers', taken with the time-keeper's office in the background. From the state of the footwear these were men whose work took them underground, and with a reminder that the excavations were carried out using illumination only from oil or acetylene lamps.*

***Left** - Tunnel shaft-head with winding gear. A wagon of spoil can be seen on the right and which has been emptied and will be repositioned ready to be sent down again.*

***Bottom** - Bonfire above the tunnel at Old Sodbury, August 1902. A contemporary newspaper report (unattributed) quotes, " During the past few weeks about a score of men have been busily engaged in building an immense bonfire, and quite 40 tons of timber and trees (supplied by W Pearson and Son, contractors of the new line, and Sir Gerald Codlington) were used in its construction, and several barrels of oil to saturate it. It was built on top of the new tunnel, at No 6 shaft, a very high peak of the Cotswold Hills. After the firing of the signal rockets on Monday night, the bonfire was successfully lighted by Miss Nash, by means of an electric magnet from the decorated arch close to Old Sodbury Vicarage grounds, and the huge pile was quickly well alight. Cornets sent forth the strains of the National Anthem, and the vast crowds of spectators took up the hymm. The bonfire was one of the largest in the kingdom, and lasted with intense brilliancy all night. Speeches were delivered by Mr H Perrett and Mr D Smith, apologising for the absence of the Rev Canon Nash, who, unfortunately, was unwell, and thanking the Coronation Festivities Committee and Mr A W Manton (agent of the works), who had so generously assisted to make the event a memorable one. Everyone rejoiced to hear the King was making satisfactory progress, and right heartily sang 'God Save the King'.*

***Right** - Mainly manual excavation at an unknown location. The temporary bridge overhead is interesting, to maintain a footpath or access or perhaps even to carry one of the many minor watercourses that dissect the railway in a north-south direction. The purpose of the stationary steam engine is not reported but it is clearly working hard - a pump perhaps? There would not appear to be any form of insulation around the firebox or boiler.*

One of a number of Hunslet 0-6-0ST locomotives used by the contractors. The mixed buffers of conventional type with massive oak baulks between will be noted. Notice also the inclined way on the right and what could well be a water wagon on top of the cutting side.

GARTH

RUSSIA

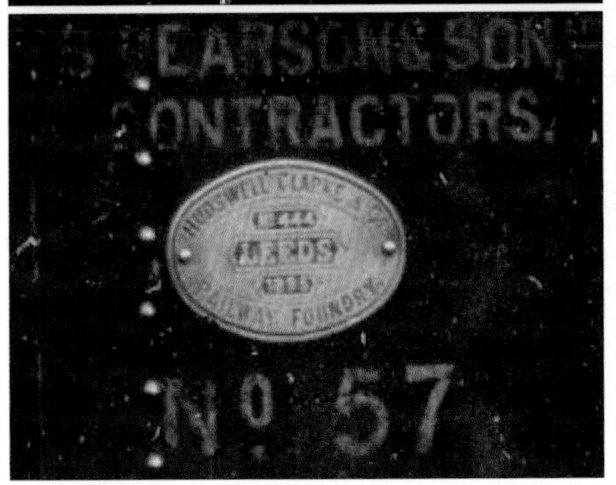

***Opposite top** - 'Garth', a Manning Wardle 0-6-0ST of 1895. (S Pearson & Son No 48.) It is believed locomotives were operated by dedicated crews, who besides working on the footplate would also be involved in maintenance and, when necessary, re-railing. The smart and clean livery will be noted, although the actual colours involved are not known.*

***Opposite bottom** - 'Russia', this time an 0-6-0ST of Hunslet build and again dating from 1895. Most of the 0-6-0 tank engines involved in the work were of this type. The engine is at the head of what could well be GWR wagons loaded with sleepers and could well be leaving one of the contractors' yards - possibly Wapley.*

***Above** - 'Sam', No 57 in the fleet, this time an 0-4-0ST of Hudswell Clarke build and also from 1895. The attached wagon is also of interesting and was probably used for inspection trips - the workmen would hardly warrant any form of protection when being transported from site to site. Most of the steam engines used on the contract (at least 42 have been identified, not all neceassarily remaining full-term, and there may well have been others) were of recent build, some as late as 1898 and so possible acquired in connection with the work. With one exception, all were also to the standard gauge.*

Opposite page - *Special duty for one of the Manning Wardle 0-6-0ST locomotives on what is clearly an inspection train of sorts seen here at Chipping Sodbury. (The identity of the engine cannot be ascertained with 100% certainty.) Graham Carpenter has been able to identify and provide detail on what is a pair of Engineering Department Saloons to Diagram Q7. "Although at first glance similar in appearance to saloons that might be hired to the public, they are in fact to Eng. Dept. Saloons. In June 1872 two Saloon Carriages were built on Lot 144 and given running numbers 715/716. At some time prior to the photograph (c.1902/3), they were modified for the Engineers' Department, this included the fitting of Guards' Lookouts. In the 1907 carriage renumbering scheme (up to this time each different class/type of carriage was numbered from 1 upwards. Saloons being renumbered in the 90xx, 91xx, 92xx and 93xx series), they were renumbered 9219/9220. Later No 9220 was again renumbered 80943 in the Eng. Dept. series. About 1910 the Carriage Diagram Index was set up (the one for wagons preceding this) and Saloon 715 was given the Diagram G.28 and 716 taking G.29 (there was only ever the one vehicle to each diagrams. Diagram numbers were issued sequentially for the next different but similar type vehicle. Sometimes these differences would be quite small, as in this case). Probably when they were renumbered into the Eng. Dept. series their diagram was changed to Q.7. (Q Diagrams covered – Inspection and Observation Saloons).*

Unfortunately somebody in the Swindon Drawing Office has conscientiously covered over some details, probably referring to 9219 after its condemnation, which may have given further details. The only difference I can spot on examining the picture is there is no ventilator over the middle small window at the rear of the first carriage but there is on the second saloon. This could be explained by the fact the view is of both sides of identical vehicles. On the first it is a corridor window while on the second carriage it is the toilet window. Other details that are identical for both vehicles are their size: 27' 6" x 8' 0" x 7' x 2"; wb 16' 0"; Lot ordered /8/1875 on renewals; the only difference is the tare weight No 715 being 10.7.0 and 716 being 9.18.2, a difference in the tare weight would not qualify for a different diagram number being issued, but what would is the fitting of a different piece of standard or special equipment. Withdrawal dates for both are not confirmed, although it is known No 9219 was condemned in 1928."

On 2 February 1903 the 'Bristol Times' carried an article describing the new, 'London,& Bristol and South Wales Direct Line'. Under the heading 'Official Inspection', it reported, "Officials representing the chief departments of the Great Western Railway spent yesterday making an inspection of the new London and Bristol and South Wales Direct Line. The examination was a thorough one, and the result was eminently satisfactory. A special train, consisting of two coaches, ran from Swindon to Patchway, taking five hours on the journey. The train stopped at every station and the heads of departments alighted and examined the buildings, the permanent way, points and crossings, the sidings, the goods yards, the signalling apparatus, signals, and the cabins. The weather was exceptionally fine, hence the inspection was made under the most favourable conditions.

"We have several times made reference to the new line in our columns, consequently readers of the 'Times and Mirror' must be thoroughly familiar with the details of the work. Now that is approaching completion, and one can travel over the railway from end to end, the character of the line can be better understood and appreciated. Three features particularly command notice - the magnitude of the undertaking, the bountiful provision made for future expansion, and the solidity of everything. The rails are laid with great accuracy and nicety, the lines and curves being admirable in their symmetry - as perfect almost as if they were drawn on paper with the aid of a rule and compass. The running lines are double, and at most of the stations there are three or four roads, to enable slow trains to set down and take up passengers without material delay while express trains are also running.

"There are seven stations on the new railway, in this order, from Wootton Bassett: - Brinkworth, Little Somerford, Hullavington, Badminton, Chipping Sodbury, Coalpit Heath and Winterbourne. At all of them the accommodation for passengers is perfect; the provision for goods traffic is abundant, and there are facilities to cope with particular business, such as for instance, the carriage of horses to and from the hunting district of Badminton. There is no passenger station at Stoke Gifford, through which the new line runs (that village being already well served by Patchway and Filton), but at this spot there are several miles of sidings. Stoke Gifford will be the marshalling place for goods trains from Bristol and Avonmouth, hence the construction of so huge a depot.

"Promise has been given - not a definite one - that the new line will be open for goods traffic at the end of March or the beginning of April. There are, however, some unforeseen difficulties which may cause a later date to be fixed. Between Badminton and the Sodbury tunnel there is a deep cutting, and the earth being of a treacherous nature it is being walled up. Then, between Coalpit Heath and Winterbourne, there is an immense embankment, constructed of soft material, that has been slipping from time to time; and considerable labour must be expended upon making it firm before even goods trains can pass over the line at this point. If the railway may not be opened, at the date set down, trains will be able to pass via Wootton Bassett and Patchway, to each end of the weak link. Every effort is being made to bring the work to a termination as early as possible, as the line is becoming more urgently needed to cope with the ever-increasing traffic of the Great Western Railway. It is claimed by the managers that the new line will serve Bristol quite as well as South Wales. Much of the passenger and goods traffic will be carried over it, and the present trunk railway being thus relieved of some of the superabundant business, there being no greater scope for augmenting the services of trains between London and the Capital of the West."

Problems on the old one...!

Aftermath of the accident at Loughor. The underside of No 1664 is indicated, whilst 'Montreal' remains upright and facing the original direction of travel. It was indeed fortuitous that no train was approaching in the opposite direction. As a result of the accident, the permanent way on the down line was distorted for a distance of some 70 yards. This damage was reported as not having been caused by No 1664 but instead by the overturning of the tender from 'Montreal', the crumpling of the underframe of the first coach and the derailment of next three coaches. Damage to the track on the up side consisted of 72 broken sleepers and 100 broken chairs, a further 30 sleepers were slightly damaged. 18 rails from the up line were 'broken'.

The safety record of the Great Western Railway was an enviable one. Between 1904 and 1937 and including the war years from 1914 - 1918, just eight passengers lost their lives whilst travelling on GWR trains*. If one were to discount the first year in question 1904, then this figure would be just five. Unfortunately it had been in 1904 when the tragic accident at Loughor had taken place. The three deaths that resulted were the most that would be killed until the Norton Fitzwarren accident 36 years later in 1940.

Loughor was unusual in that despite a meticulous investigation of the scene including permanent way, signalling, locomotives and rolling stock, no definite conclusion as to the cause was ever found. Similarly the evidence of the surviving locomen failed to shed light on a cause whilst the weather was likewise not considered to have played a part. What conclusions that were reached by the Coroner and Lt.Col. H A Yorke, the Board of Trade Inspector were compelling but not necessarily final, and consequently Loughor may be said to be a rare example where we never fully know the reason why three persons plus two locomen died.

Loughor itself is on the main line west of Llanelly.

* This figure does not include accidents to passengers on lines later taken over by the GWR but which were independent prior to 1923. Neither does it include fatalities to railway staff. Fatalities that might have occurred to persons, passengers / trespassers / railway staff are similarly not included, neither are those cases involving injuries. See also later in this work referring to the Slough accident.

Around 1.20pm on 3 October 1904 the 10.35am passenger service from New Milford (later Neyland) to Paddington was running east near to Loughor station when it became derailed. (Contemporary newspaper reports refer to the service having the name of the 'Flying Welshman'. The train consisted of two engines, the train engine a member of the 'Bulldog' class, No 3460 'Montreal', whilst at Llanelly 0-6-0ST No 1664 of the '1661' class had been attached as pilot to assist the train over Cockett bank. Both engines were running chimney first. Behind the tender of 'Montreal' were eight bogie passenger vehicles and at the end a 6-wheel milk van. The total weight of the rolling stock was put at 196 tons, the train 'well-filled' with an estimated 300 passengers. The accident happened on a slight embankment on straight and level track, the permanent way having been inspected that same morning and found to be in good order.

It was whilst on this section that the pilot engine, No 1664 became derailed, eventually coming to rest on its right hand side having turned through 180° to straddle the opposite, down, line. The front bogie of No 3460 meanwhile was similarly derailed, but remained facing east although the tender was swung around. Fortunately the driving wheels of No 3460 remained on the track.

As a result of No 1664 becoming derailed, the coupling severed between the two engines likewise the vacuum brake pipe. The latter caused an immediate full brake application but (and as Col. Yorke commented), this would have taken five to six seconds to take effect at the rear of the train with the result that initially at least, the full weight of the train was still travelling forward complete with its kinetic energy, although this momentum and its associated force was decreasing all the time.

One of the facts considered was the speed, neither engine having a speedometer. As a result any estimate could only be based on the time of the train when passing various signal boxes as well as the opinion of the crew of 'Montreal', the crew of No 1664 being killed in the accident. Notwithstanding differing opinions expressed, the conclusion was the speed was in the order of 60 mph.

One aspect that was at one time thought to have been contributory was a broken coupling rod on the right hand side of No 1664. However there were no marks on the sleepers to indicate this had failed beforehand and it was subsequently discounted as the cause.

As mentioned earlier, no tracks and rolling stock defects were found, 'Montreal' was minutely examined and found to be in excellent condition. Outside forces including those of a third-party were evidently not considered worthy of mention in the official report.

What was left to consider was speed and stability

The first vehicle of the train, No 2927 a bogie-third. It came to rest minus its underframe at the foot of the embankment on the down line. All the other vehicles remained on the up side. The accident was first reported by the fireman of No 3460 to the signalman on duty at Loughor signal box, a distance of about one mile from the crash site. Despite being at the very least shocked as a result, he covered this distance in the very commendable time of around seven minutes. Already a crane may be seen at work.

and in the latter case the focus came to rest on No 1664 which could have been being pushed by No 3460. In evidence various drivers gave the view that had this been the case then the stability of No 1664 would have been even better. (Col. Yorke appeared unconvinced but this view was not proceeded further.) The stability of an outside-frame tank engine travelling at this speed including its centre of gravity was the subject of some debate although the driver of No 3460 recounted that just before the accident he had observed the driver and fireman of No 1664 apparently seated and certainly not appearing to show signs of concern over the riding of No 1664. Col. Yorke, though, could not accept this comment. He was of the opinion that the driver of an express train would be unlikely to be seated whilst from his own position, the driver of 'Montreal' would have been unable to see if the fireman on No 1664 was seated. Maintenance records indicated, No 1664 had received a general overhaul in late 1903 only returning to traffic in January 1904. Since that time it had only amassed a further 15,000 miles and was considered to be in excellent mechanical condition.

In conclusion it was left to the view that No 1664 had initially derailed due to the speed involved, possibly because of weight transference or oscillation set up due to the amount of water being carried. No less a person than G J Churchward gave evidence that he considered the riding of a tank engine of the type to be perfectly acceptable at speed, but Col. Yorke was not convinced and made recommendations that when a pilot engine were deemed necessary it should ideally be of the tender type or if a tank engine were to be used a strict lower speed limit be enforced, this limit to be set below the preferred maximum of 50mph (40 mph was indicated), so as to take into account the different opinions as to speed of individual locomen.

Notwithstanding the debris that resulted, one track was restored to traffic (we are not told which one) the same day.

The second and third vehicles of the London train, respectively No 1227: a corridor brake tri-composite and No 3178: a corridor third. The damage to these vehicles was reported as, "Second carriage: underframe bent and side of body smashed, Third carriage: three compartments at one end smashed." In the background outside frame 0-6-0 No 677 has arrived to assist whilst standing on the embankment is a hand-operated crane.

SMOKING

Two further views of 'Bulldog' class engines, Nos 3465 'Trinidad' and 3458 'Natal Colony' recorded at New Milford. In the top view one of the men is reported as 'Engineman Jefferies'.

Both Great Western Trust.

Coaches in Colour

One of ten third-class saloons, Nos 9101 to 9110, built in 1929 to Diagram G58 and Lot No 1400. All are shown as entering service on 4 May 1929 and were 58ft 4½ins long by 9ft wide. Michael Harris refers to them as 'Nondescript Brake Saloons' - literally meaning 'class-less'. They were built for private-hire and excursion work, being similar to earlier Toplight saloons. Inside were inward facing bench seats and Edwardian mahogany woodwork with folding tables - Harris states the latter restricted movement. There was also a single passenger compartment identical with contemporary side-corridor coaches. By the 1950s BR standard open-third stock meant that the 1929 vehicles found a new use as brake vehicles either end of the WR's then five sets of excursion stock. They were displaced from this when BR open brake-thirds arrived on the scene. Even so, they survived on general and excursion work as late as 1961 but all had been condemned by the middle of 1962. No W9103W found final use in a television exhibition train and as a result lasted long enough to be preserved. It is now on the Severn Valley Railway.

Final days for a 1906 'Concertina' Brake-Third, No W3494W, seen having its wheels tapped at Swindon whilst at the head of a Paddington-Bristol-Weston-super-Mare train. This vehicle was one of ten built in January 1907 to Diagram D43, Lot No 1120 and were a massive 70ft x 9ft in size. As built they had gas lighting and hammered glass over the droplights - although in this BR view the former has at least been updated. Earlier, 15 similar vehicles had been built to the same diagram in 1906. All the brake-third vehicles of Concertina type were withdrawn by 1956, some of their last duties being on Paddington to Neyland services. Consequently the view here, with the coach coupled to a new BR Mk1, must be a rare occasion. It is perhaps interesting to speculate on the number of liveries carried by this vehicle over the years; starting with ornate crimson-lake, through to the 1912 chocolate and cream, possibly all brown post 1914, then a revival of the ornate style in 1922, followed by a simpler style in 1927. A return again to all-brown post-1939 and possibly a repaint in plain chocolate and cream after 1945. The BR livery seen would have been the last it carried.

W 6610 W
GUARD

7445

The Fairford branch was a 22 mile railway from Yarnton passing through Witney (the original terminus) and then continuing via Brize Norton and Bampton, Carterton, Alverscot, Kelmscott and Langford, Lechlade, to the terminus at Fairford albeit a mile or so from the village of the same name. The original intention had been to reach Cheltenham hence the continuation of the railway for a short distance beyond the station at Fairford but which piece was only ever used as the goods yard and for engine facilities. Opened in 1873, the terminus and indeed the intermediate stations were never likely to generate much in the way of revenue, the exception being at Witney where there was the addition of the renowned blanket manufacturer. Even so the railway managed to retain its passenger service until 1962, freight lingering on at Witney just into the next decade.

Fortunately the late Mark Warburton visited the line in its last full year of operation, 1961. In the views opposite, 57xx 0-6-0PTs, Nos 9653 and 7445 are seen on passenger stock and by the turntable respectively, 11 March 1961. The liveries of the locomotives and stock may have changed since 1948 but at least the conical water tower still displays the colours of the old company. In the yard the siding is mainly occupied by mineral wagons, coal being the mainstay of traffic by this time, and mainly intended for domestic use. According to one source (S C Jenkins), passenger traffic at Fairford had dwindled to no more than a dozen regular users by the time of closure.

Notwithstanding its length, tank engines were a regular feature on the line, supplemented by members of the 22xx type on occasions. (Like at least one other cross-country route the Didcot, Newbury & Southampton line, the Fairford line was worked by single-wheeler 2-2-2 tender engines of the 'Queen' class prior to WW1, one of their last duties.) The provision of a turntable (reported as having been either 45' or 55' diameter) at Fairford also meant engines were invariably turned before returning to Oxford. Notice in the lower view how the concrete lamp standard has deteriorated, the concrete having broken away to expose the reinforcing.

In the view on this page, Mark has captured a train near Fairford on the same date, pannier tank No 7412 in charge of two passenger coaches and a former LMS full-brake.

Mark Warburton, courtesy Mrs Margaret Warburton.

Above - Still on the Fairford branch but this time at Lechlade, the first station east of Fairford. No 9653 is leaving for Oxford, running parallel with the goods loop, on 11 March 1961. The vehicles are by Messrs Collett and Hawksworth, those of the latter especially quickly downgraded from front-line duty by the influx of the inferior BR Mk1 design. The railway was by now some 88 years old, and whilst there is evidence of 'modern' GWR/WR practice, liveries of course but also the concrete fencing and tubular signal posts with metal arms, much would still be recognisable as GWR to those from earlier years. We may ponder on the thoughts of the guard as he observes the photographer, within a year passengers would cease, an accelerating pace of change and this even before the infamous doctor arrived on the scene.... .

Opposite top - South and west of the Fairford line were the two short branches from Kemble to Cirencester and also to Tetbury. Both were early users of 4-wheel railbuses intended to reduce operating costs as well as provide a service to intermediate stopping points. AC railbus No W79977 is at the junction station of Kemble on 14 May 1960 the destination indicating a service to the GWR terminus at Cirencester Town. (Cirencester had a second station 'Watermoor' on the north-south MSWJ route.) For a time the introduction of the railbus service appeared as if it might indeed save the railway but it was to no avail and despite much investment in new rebuilding of the terminus at Cirencester as late as 1956, passenger services were withdrawn on 4 April 1964 and all traffic 18 months later.

Opposite bottom - Also running from Kemble was a 7 mile branch to Tetbury, another line on which railbuses of the type seen were introduced as a means of reducing costs. Whilst the light weight of these vehicles might at first glance be seen as an opportunity to reduce maintenance, at this period the railway was still compelled to act as a 'common carrier', meaning it had to take whatever freight was offered and which in turn meant steam engines, heavier than a railbus, were still required. (In 1963 it was reported that the complete live and deadstock of a local farm was transported by train from Tetbury to Stranraer in a train of 31 vehicles. This included a herd of pedigree Hereford cattle.) On what was a wet 24 February 1962, 2-6-2T No 5547 is seen on freight at the terminus, either having just arrived from Kemble or in the process of shunting vehicles in to the goods shed and yard. Closure came on the same day as the branch to Cirencester, 4 April 1964.

Mark Warburton, courtesy Mrs Margaret Warburton.

CIRENCESTER TOWN

TETBURY
15

Top - Banished by DMUs from its original intended task of working the London suburban services, 2-6-2T No 6148 leaves a smoke screen as it blasts its way past Old Mills near Radstock on 20 May 1964. The colliery here had closed just a few weeks earlier and there would be no more work for the Ruston & Hornsby diesel alongside. No 6148 would remain in service only until September 1964.

Left - The top of the Pensford colliery incline. It is believed the signal was operated from the main line Pensford and Bromley Quarry Sidings Signal Box and when 'off' indicated a wagon could be accommodated in the exchange sidings at the foot of the gradient.

Opposite page - The incline at Kilmersdon colliery near Radstock on 12 July 1968. The drop from the colliery to the line below was some 100 feet with the average gradient of the incline at 1 in 6½. 12 July 1968.

Mark Warburton, courtesy Mrs Margaret Warburton.

Right - *One of the items that started a lifetime's fascination with the (Motor) Economic System of Maintenance. Referred to in the text opposite as the 'Paddington Record', this book provides detail of all the lines on which the original Economic system operated, their lengths, position of huts, gang lengths, savings and costs.*

Bottom *- Summer at Kingsbidge, 26 August 1961. From the vantage point of West Alvington Hill, a first generation DMU leaves a haze of diesel fumes as it departs for Brent with a strengthening coach in tow. Diesel units had arrived on the branch in the Spring 1961 although this limited means of reducing costs was insufficient to forestall closure, which took place from the end of July 1963. The Kingsbridge branch was one of numerous lines maintained by the Engineering Department under the (Motor) Economic System of Maintenance the history and operation of which is described opposite.*

Cty. Mrs Margaret Warburton

The GWR Economic System of Maintenance

Pick up many of the books on GW branch and secondary routes produced in recent years and they will often refer to the Economic or (so far as later years were concerned) the Motor Economic System of Maintenance. This might well be accompanied by an extract from the relevant Sectional Appendix and possibly also a photograph or two of a ganger on a trolley of some sort. What this informs the reader is that the line in question was maintained under the (Motor) Economic System, although what is sometimes lacking is an explanation of how this system came to be developed and similarly what exactly was involved.

The concept of the system may already be known, in outline at least, to many railway devotees. For those perhaps not so informed, the system may be described as being one where a section of single line is sub-divided into small sections with a key box at intervals along that section. One key, which will fit any of the boxes in a given section, is provided and which, when withdrawn, prevents the signalman at either end from obtaining a 'token' (for 'token' read also 'tablet' or 'train-staff') and so allowing a train to pass. The ganger/men can thus work in perfect safety without the need for lookouts within the section (either walking to the requisite site or using a hand/motor trolley to reach the work site). As such economy in working is achieved with all the men in a gang able to undertake a task as against two - one either side of the work-site - needed to act as flagmen and warn of the approach of a train. When the work had been completed, the equipment is removed from the track and the key restored at any of the key boxes en-route in time for the line to be available again for the release of a 'token' to enable the passage of a train. In this way it is similar – but in no way identical to the means of operation of a single line with staff / token / tablet. The use of the words 'hand' or 'motor' referred to the 'trolley' system as it developed over the years, the development of motor trolleys allowing the men to travel further to reach their required site of work. Even so the hand-trolley system was a great improvement on having to walk to the work-site. The occupation-key system was also refined over the years and whilst originally corresponding exactly with the token lengths, it was later extended so that the ganger's sphere of occupation might well overlap token sections. This necessitated the use of what was then state of the art technology in the form of occupation control instruments as are referred to later.

Having described the principles we need to travel back to the turn of the 20th century and when there was concern over maintenance costs on lines having a limited train service and consequent limited revenue. There were a number of minor branch lines where the permanent-way was maintained by several gangs of perhaps 3-4 men each responsible for a short section of line and whose only mechanical assistance was in the form of a push-trolley onto which heavy items might be placed and so rolled to the requisite site of work. Similarly it was the practice for the ganger to have occupation of the line between set periods

Purported as taken at Witney on the Fairford branch, a posed view of four members of the p/way gang with a hand trolley. Similar vehicles would probably have been in use from the earliest days of railways and enabled men to move cumbersome items, in this case sleepers, from a local stockpile to the required site of work. The obvious disadvantages were timing and safety, timing in so far as fitting the movement in between trains and safety because of the need to have flagmen and detonators either side of the final worksite in order to protect the workforce and warn approaching trains. Although four men are shown, there would have been two more, on either side of the location acting as the lookouts. GWR Official.

An image which has appeared elsewhere but perhaps not accounting for the significance it displays. Again it is an official posed view also on the Fairford/Witney line: notice the inside keyed track. The individual concerned would seem to be one of the same men seen on the previous page. Here technology has provided him with a 'geared' hand operated 'velocipede' with which to inspect his length - the gearing comes from the two sets of handles, the lower set used for faster transit. Movement was achieved by a fore and aft action, although even so muscles were required. A key hammer and fishplate spanner will be noted attached to the cross member. There was no springing whilst movement across facing points could often result in a derailment. In order to use the vehicle to inspect the line in safety some form of security was required, either possession of the token (staff/tablet) or an occupation key. If the former, the inspection would have to involve movement through the whole section - or a return to the point of departure. The occupation key however allowed confidence that no train could approach, as with this in the possession of the ganger a token for a train could not be released by the signalman. The occupation key could also be restored at any one of several intermediate key boxes placed mid-section, the trolley lifted clear of the track. These key boxes were not initially equipped with a telephone and instead it is inferred in contemporary notes that the ganger would carry a portable device which he would plug into the telephone circuit. If so this could well be the very first use of a 'mobile telephone'. Might it be that the large box on the rear of the velocipede contained this portable device? From photographs, hand-propelled velocipedes came in differing types, no doubt from different manufacturers. Riding one in the face of a howling gale with the wind lashing down must have been a none too pleasant experience. *GWR Official*

each day - not a problem with a limited train service and where there were long gaps between workings. However this did cause problems if a timetabled working was late or if it was deemed necessary to run an additional service. Simply put, once the ganger had been given permission to occupy the line there would usually be no way of contacting him again, unless the work was in close proximity to a station or if a 'runner' was sent. Additional or delayed trains would then reduce the time then available for maintenance.

Initially the economic system of maintenance involved purely economy in man-power, assisted by telephone boxes at intervals along the line, there were no special signalling instruments or keys and therefore no electrical interlocking. Where the advantage came with the telephone was that communication, albeit one-sided as the signalman could not attract the attention of the ganger, was at least possible. The ganger was by now also equipped with a hand-operated trolley of some sort for inspection purposes, he could now inspect his section of line quicker and was also able to communicate with the signalman at intervals: and so be able to remove his trolley from the line if told a train was due. 'A clear understanding' - the oft-quoted phrase from the rulebook was needed between the two men, for there was nothing stopping the signalman from obtaining a 'token' (train-staff/tablet) and giving this to the driver of a train which might then proceed towards where a ganger or men were working.

Concurrent with the inspection trolley came the provision of pump-trucks operated by two/four men and which again could be lifted off the track as required. Even so when working on-site, the dangers inherent with this were obvious and in consequence it was necessary to position a flag-man either side of the site of work not only to alert the driver of an approaching train but also to warn the other men in the gang. Two members of the gang might therefore be classed as being 'unproductive' despite performing a vital service.

Contemporary modern technology was to change this situation leading to the development of the motor system being introduced in the late 1920s and which together with the original hand-trolley working formed the basis of a system which worked for over sixty years through the years of the GWR and well into the days of the Western Region. Indeed some lines retained the original hand-trolley form of maintenance right up to closure. The demise of the economic/motor-economic system came about with the closure of the lines involved and alterations (again to save cost) in regular track inspection.

As an example as to how matters progressed from the years we may look at the erstwhile Golden Valley Railway.

It was in 1899, that the GWR had acquired the 19 mile Golden Valley branch from Pontrilas to Hay. Previously worked under private ownership, the line had ceased to operate regular services as far back as 1898 but under the ownership of Paddington was restored ready for

Page 6 of the 'Paddington Record' - see illustration on p40 - referring to 'The Golden Valley Railway'. This is a typical example of the detail contained within the book and which so far as the Golden Valley Railway was concerned continues with a further two pages of detail information on costs, savings, and workings. In several places throughout the book there are references to "see bundle No.....", regretfully these bundles/papers appear not to have survived. (Note the hand written words 'Now motor' written across the page clearly indicating this line was subsequently converted from the original Economic system to the Motor Economic system. With the latter and with the ability to cover a greater distance with a motor trolley it is likely there was a further reduction in the number of staff required - a repeat of what had occurred when the original economic system had been introduced. It is a matter of regret that no similar Paddington record giving the same details but for lines equipped or converted to the Motor System has been discovered.

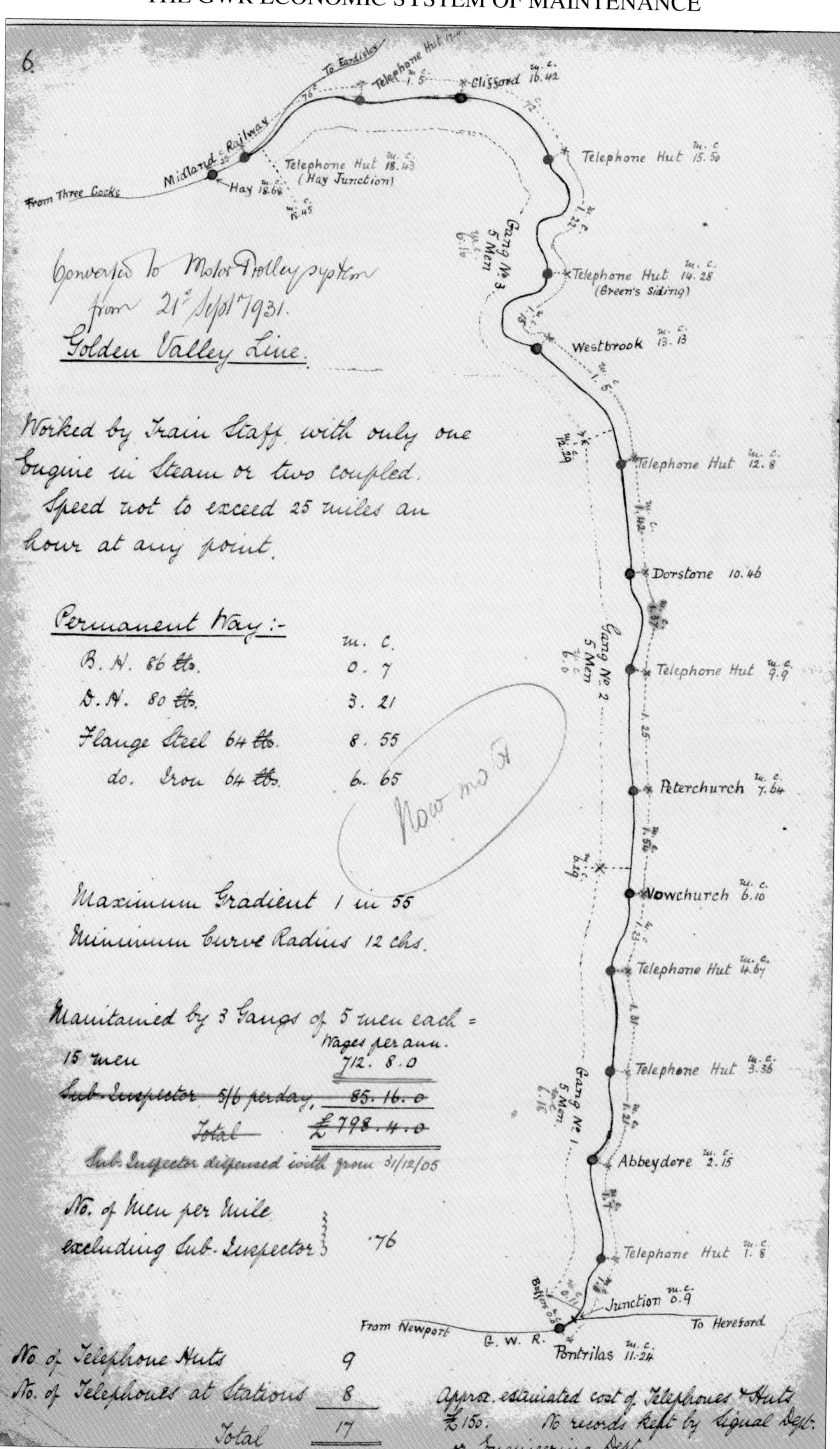

6.

Converted to Motor Trolley system from 21st Sept 1931.

Golden Valley Line.

Worked by Train Staff with only one Engine in Steam or two coupled.
Speed not to exceed 25 miles an hour at any point.

Permanent Way:-

	m. c.
B. H. 86 lbs.	0. 7
D. H. 80 lbs.	3. 21
Flange Steel 64 lbs.	8. 55
do. Iron 64 lbs.	6. 65

Now motor

Maximum Gradient 1 in 55
Minimum Curve Radius 12 chs.

Maintained by 3 Gangs of 5 men each =

	Wages per ann.
15 men	712. 8. 0
~~Sub-Inspector 5/6 per day,~~	~~85. 16. 0~~
~~Total~~	~~£ 798. 4. 0~~

~~Sub-Inspector dispensed with from 31/12/05~~

No. of Men per Mile excluding Sub-Inspector } ·76

No. of Telephone Huts	9
No. of Telephones at Stations	8
Total	17

Approx. estimated cost of Telephones & Huts £150. No records kept by Signal Dept. or Engineering Dept.

From a contemporary technical journal a view of a wayside telephone and occupation-key hut. (Why the portable telephone system was dispensed with is unknown - weight/ reliability perhaps, unless there were also fixed telephones at certain locations as well?) The hut is simple yet functional, its purpose only to provide weather protection to the equipment within - notice the 'T' plate on the exterior. It is not thought the actual huts were ever fitted with cast plates identifying a particular location. Inset: the ganger is at one of the early key-instruments this being of the circular type. A fixed telephone is on the wall nearby - did the men have to receive instructions how to use a telephone?. The location is not stated and it will be noted there is no velocipede or run-off point shown. The circular key instrument and its use is described on p49.

reopening on Wednesday May 1st 1901. Paddington could never have been in any doubt as to the limited return the railway would generate and it would appear that even before re-opening took place the line was selected as the guinea-pig for what would become the Economic System of Maintenance. According to the *Railway Gazette*, the genus for economy in operation of single lines in the manner to be described, originated from Mr. – afterwards Sir – James Inglis, Chief Engineer of the GWR from 1892 to 1903 and then General Manager from 1903 to 1911.

In so far as the train service on the Golden Valley single line was concerned, the route was operated as one single section throughout, the driver having with him a wooden train staff (in this case round in shape and painted red) as his authority to proceed. An Annett's key was provided at the end of the staff to unlock various

A mechanical pump-trolley. Whilst examples have been seen with short handles for use by just two men, this one has four handles and so may have been the type involved if a trailer was involved to carry tools and equipment. The pump action connected directly to the wheels with no 'free-wheel' facility. It is not known if brakes were at first provided although this was certainly a consideration later. The trolleys could be manhandled off the track on to a short section of track as per the gangers' inspection trolley although four men would be needed. Whilst there appears to be a manufacturers plate provided, this cannot be accurately read - possibly the origins were in America with the firm of 'Buda', the same firm from where it believed some of the first inspection trolleys were purchased. Again the view is taken from a technical journal with no clue given as to the location although the obvious gradient will be noted. (Gradients and head-winds were a consideration as to whether a line was considered suitable for hand-trolleys.)

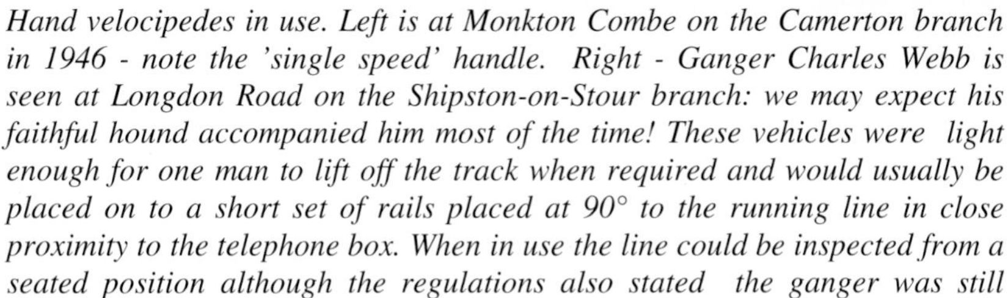

Hand velocipedes in use. Left is at Monkton Combe on the Camerton branch in 1946 - note the 'single speed' handle. Right - Ganger Charles Webb is seen at Longdon Road on the Shipston-on-Stour branch: we may expect his faithful hound accompanied him most of the time! These vehicles were light enough for one man to lift off the track when required and would usually be placed on to a short set of rails placed at 90° to the running line in close proximity to the telephone box. When in use the line could be inspected from a seated position although the regulations also stated the ganger was still expected to walk the section weekly. It should be noted that not all the lines that were originally equipped for the economic system of maintenance using hand-trolleys were subsequently up-graded to the 'motor' system. Hence hand-operated velocipedes and mechanical pump-trolleys continued in use well into BR days. Mr Webb was unfortunately killed near Longdon Road on 3 February 1930 when his trolley was hit from behind by the engine of a goods train. The Ministry of Transport enquiry into the tragedy revealed the goods train was running 15 minutes ahead of time allied to which Ganger Webb did not contact the signalman by telephone to ascertain if the line was clear. The formal conclusion was that this was a case where non-compliance with the laid-down rules resulted in the accident. It also highlighted the inherent weakness in the 'Telephone System of Maintenance' whereby there was nothing stopping a train being despatched. The later development and provision of an occupation key, the release of which locked the system so no staff/token could be issued to a service train, would prevent similar accidents. Even so the point to note is that by 1930 the occupation-key variation had been in use for many years, yet there still remained minor branches where installation was still pending, or as here where telephone maintenance was retained due to the very light traffic.
Colin Maggs collection and Kidderminster Railway Museum, Lane collection

intermediate ground frames en-route. Train operation on the branch required each service to carry the actual staff: the 'One engine in steam principle'. 'Staff and ticket working' was not permitted.

As it existed, any necessary track or lineside maintenance - where the latter encroached upon the running line - could only be undertaken when flagmen (with detonators) were provided as a means of warning. These flagmen – or lookouts, were positioned according to the visibility appertaining to the location of the work, usually in the order of three-quarters of a mile either side and as such afforded the requisite braking/warning distance to an approaching train. In addition to this was the loss of time involved with the Ganger and men having to walk to and from the nearest signal box to the place of work at the beginning and end of every intended occupation of the line.

The new arrangement saw the installation of 17 telephone huts over the 19 mile route, eight of these were at the intermediate stations and the remaining nine at various points in-between. The spacing of the huts in relation to the existing stations meant that at no point on the line would a ganger be ever more than 67 chains (1,474 yards or just over 0.83 of a mile) from a telephone.

The actual working arrangements are summarised within the Paddington record, "Between 6.0 am and 5.30 pm there are five regular and four occasional trains. The line is examined throughout daily by a Sub-Inspector using a light velocipede inspection car. He also does the usual Inspector's work in connection with Time Sheets and Stock and other Returns on the Golden Valley Railway". (The times stated were consistent throughout the Paddington book and did not include trains running outside this period. The reason for this was simply in Rule 215c "A trolley must be used only during daylight and when the weather is sufficiently

Near Todenham Road Level Crossing on the Shipston branch, 'Telephone Hut No 1'. Note there is no obvious provision for a trolley run-off. At some point in time guards of trains on branch lines (whether this applied to all branch lines and when it was introduced is not known) were issued with a key allowing access to the telephone huts. This certainly applied to the installation on the former MSWJ route. By inference, the telephone huts were kept locked.

Roger Carpenter

clear….".) Each Ganger is provided with a watch: and Mechanical Trolleys (sic) are provided for the Gangs. (Contemporary records for the Golden Valley Railway refer to three gangs of five men in each with a total wage bill of £712 8s per annum. Added to this was the Sub Inspectors wage of 5/6d daily, making £85 16s per annum, or a grand total of £798 4s.)

Under the original method before the introduction of telephone huts, the line was regarded as being in the occupation of the Permanent Way men between certain specified times each day and the Gangers had to go to the nearest telephone huts, to report 'Line Clear' (to the signalbox at either end of the line) ready for the next train". With the mention of the four 'occasional trains' it may be assumed that these were run as required to suit traffic needs. However, this means of operation would have prevented any of these 'occasional trains' running at short notice although it must be said there is no record of any undue delay having been occasioned. Presumably then there must also have been excellent liaison between the station masters, signalmen, and gangers?

As such this is the first recorded use of a 'velocipede' inspection car, and whilst it is a matter of regret that no photograph of such a vehicle survives on the line, what is believed to be an identical vehicle was recorded elsewhere as per the image on page 42.

With the line then considered 'under occupation' at certain times, the use of flagmen could be dispensed with. The note as to the provision of a watch to each ganger is of interest in so far as the artisan of the period would have been unlikely to have otherwise possessed such an item. Interestingly also, despite the obvious novelty of the equipment and general installation, the record for costs is limited. The Paddington record states, "Approx estimated cost of Telephone Huts £150. No records kept by Signal Dept. or Engineering Dept."

Few photographs of these telephone huts appear to have survived - slightly surprising in light of the thousands of images taken by the GWR official photographer - one is shown on this page. They would appear to have been of simple timber build and probably intended to afford weather protection to the telephone itself rather than the user, (unless they were positioned to coincide with the siteing of a permanent way hut?). It is not thought there would have been any facility for the signal box to "call" the ganger, indeed unless work was being undertaken in the immediate vicinity of the telephone box, there would have been little point. At the stations the telephones would no doubt have been located in a convenient building.

Such then were the facilities for the Golden Valley line although this type of working was destined to be somewhat short lived. Indeed just 15 months later, on Monday 11th August 1902 change took place in the Rules and is again described by the Paddington record, "In accordance with amended instructions, the Gangers obtain occupation by telephone when they require it and only report 'Line Clear' after obtaining permission for an occupation (meaning they report when the line is clear for traffic). This saves the Gangers a good deal of walking". This modification would no doubt have assisted in the running of the 'as required' services, a ganger upon enquiring as to availability for occupation being able to be told if a train was due.

What this meant was that the next step in the development of the system had just taken place, with occupation considered to occur on demand rather than as a predetermined belief. Of course in either case the use of telephones alone still did not prevent the physical issue of the train staff although there would have been strict instructions for the commencement (and termination) of periods of occupation to be recorded within the signal box Train Register.

Moving on slightly in the history of the Golden Valley Railway, it is worth recounting that two further entries refer to the line. The first states that, "On 1st January 1906 Sub-Inspector S. Jenkin was transferred to the Severn & Wye Joint Line (Northern Section) and the gangers were each provided with a Velocipede Car to enable them to inspect their own lengths daily." "Mr. G.W. Blackall (believed to have been the Divisional Engineer for the Gloucester area. Was he related to the A.T. Blackall referred

Table 1- The first installations – telephone maintenance.

Route / Branch	Route Length (maintained length in brackets)	Introduction of system	Type of rail originally provided	Number of telephones	Minimum radius curve (chains)	Maximum Gradient 1 in	Cost	Estimated Original Saving per annum	Note
Golden Valley	18m 52ch (19.75 ½)	1-5-1901	B.N.? & Flange	17	12	55	£150	£151 13s 4d	Converted to 'Motor' 21-9-1931
Wrington Vale	6m 41 ch (7m 43ch)	4-12-1901	Vignole	9	14	50	£75	£106 12s	
Culm Valley	7m 29ch (7m 76ch)	30-5-1904	Vignole	11	6	67	£94 11s 9d	£105 6s	

to later?), estimates that had this Branch been maintained under Standard Rules the following Staff would have been needed: "Four gangs of five men each, and which allowing for the saving then of five men is £151.13s 4d per annum. Further saving when Sub-Inspector dispensed with and meaning gross saving per annum now of £237 9s 4d." – from the figures given it appears the saving for the loss of Inspector Jenkin is given as £85 16s per annum, exactly the same amount as per when his salary was referred to in 1901. From a social perspective alone this would also indicate that there was then no such thing as an annual wage increment.

We may conclude then that the year 1901 had seen that despite the limited installation of the scheme on the Golden Valley it had quickly proven the concept of economy in track maintenance and as such the scheme was expanded to another route even before the end of the same year. Again though, it was a cautious move as it involved the little Wrington Vale Light Railway running east from Congresbury Junction near Yatton and which as was reported when opened on 4th December 1901, was also provided with the Economic System already in place.

As with the previous Golden Valley Railway, the Wrington Vale route was similarly operated by 'one engine in steam' (- or two coupled together), and was reported as having ten regular trains daily. Perhaps surprisingly it was categorically stated there were no additional occasional workings. As before the details of the installation and advice of the actual equipment refer to a total of nine telephones, five in the signal boxes at the stations and four in intermediate huts (- once again the reference refers to "No records kept", but gives an "approx estimate" of £75 and which includes the cost of four huts. The maximum distance between any telephone was one mile two chains. Again the record affords an idea of the cost involved and with the perceived cost in this case of £106 12s per annum compared with what would have been the additional number of men required for ordinary maintenance, the economic system referring to an annual wage bill of £357.10 for seven men.

Interestingly in so far as the Wrington Vale Light Railway was concerned, the route was referred to as being examined by a Foreman Platelayer daily on the light velocipede car rather then the Ganger. Both these men were provided with watches by the GWR.

On 1st April 1904 a special notice is referred to as having been issued and stating, "No trolley to be put on the line until permission has been obtained by telephone from the nearest Station". Clearly this would appear to have been a basic requirement and so may very well refer to a specific incident that had occurred. Unfortunately no further details are given.

The system remained in use on the branch until closure to passengers on 14th September 1931 at which time the Wrington Vale Gang, No 142, was disbanded. Maintenance was then transferred to the nearby Cheddar Valley Branch Gang, No 141, and whose strength was reported as being increased by two lengthmen as a result. (The fate of the displaced men is not reported).

Ahead in time, but concluding the story of the system on the Wrington Vale route, a further note of 7th September 1940 indicated that much of the working had changed little over the years, "The Velocipede Car and Mechanical Trolley are still in use. The Ganger examines the length once a week, walking one way and returning by Velocipede car - other days a lengthman examines the length. Two lengthmen attached to the main gang are employed whole time on the Branch and the Ganger takes the whole gang there when necessary. The telephones have been removed from the huts – the only ones remaining being at Wrington, Langford, and Blagdon Stations". (Clearly a mechanical trolley had been provided at some time after 1904 and as is referred to under the next heading of the Culm Valley Branch, this could have been supplied very early on. In so far as the Wrington Vale Light Railway is concerned no other details are given).

The final line to be considered at this stage is the little Culm Valley Branch in Devon running just over 7¼ miles from a connection with the Bristol to Exeter line at Tiverton Junction to the terminus at Hemyock. As with the first installation on the Golden Valley route, the Culm Valley line was another that had been taken over by the GWR. The light permanent way of 1904 (Vignole rail of just 75lbs per yard) meant that the maximum axle loading was set at eight tons and speed was restricted to 15 miles an hour. Their was a maximum of six trains daily between 6.0 am and 5.30 pm.

A total of 11 telephones were provided at a maximum distance of 73 chains (1,606 yards) apart. Seven of these were in huts and the remaining four at the termini/ intermediate stations.

The system was brought into use from 30th May 1904 (the Culm Valley line had been maintained by the GWR from as early as 1878 and was taken over by the GWR in August 1880. This time also the costings and equipment

A standard occupation-key instrument with key inserted. Note this is an official view and the key is a blank yet to be engraved. At some stage this type of machine replaced the circular design: when and why is not known. Likewise it is not known if circular machines were then retained at their original locations. (Certainly by the mid 1930's the design seen here was the type of preference.) The wording on both this and the circular type was identical, 'To obtain key after receiving signalman's permission, turn key to No 2 & wait until space indicated 'free' then turn key to No 3. To replace key turn to No 1'. The numbers would appear in the circular dial and the word 'Free' in the slot at the top. Note the key shown is of 'A' configuration - representing 'half past nine o'clock'. Keys could be made to one of five configurations 'A' through to 'E'. Because of the design of the key there was no 'master' available and so a key would only fit into a machine within its 'group'. Adjacent occupation key sections had keys to different configurations. In service the keys were engraved, "Possession of this key authorises ganger to occupy the line between..........", the engraving filled with black wax. The same type of instrument was also used as a ground frame release instrument but in this case the key slot was larger, keys were not interchangeable between the two. At some stage, possibly in recent years, the phrase 'tombstone' instrument', taken from the curved top design has been referred to. To prevent unauthorised interference with the mechanism, the instrument was locked by a metal bar passing through the base and cover attached to which was a padlock. One feature that was not carried over to the 'tombstone' type from the early circular instruments, was that a hammer hit the inside of the metal case as the free indicator was displayed, this then gave an audible indication that the key was able to be released. (A release and the presence of the 'Free' indication which in turn released the electric lock within, was obtained by the signalman at either end of the section holding down their ringing key simultaneously.)

were more detailed. For the telephones and huts the amount stated was £71 5s 9d added to which were a Velocipede Car: £10, Mechanical Trolley: £11 5s, and watch: £2 1s. A total of £94 11s 9d. (The watch is of interest in that its value was considerably more than the Ganger's weekly wage. At that time a Sub-Inspector received 5/6d daily and a Foreman Platelayer 4/9d. Between the two the grade of Ganger would have been likely to be on a rate in the order of 5/- per day with each man working the then standard six-day week.)

This is also the first time there is a direct reference to the provision of a Mechanical Trolley (what type?), although it would be reasonable to assume then that such an item was also provided on the other two lines previously mentioned - for 'mechanical' read 'hand-operated'. The Culm Valley branch was maintained by a single gang of seven men at a total wage bill of £326 6s per annum. The Paddington accountants calculated that a saving of £105 6s was possible per year under the economic system and which was the equivalent of two men per year. In this way the installation would be considered to have paid for itself in less than a year. Statistically too they also refer to the number of men per mile involved in maintenance, and which was 1.13 under standard rules and 0.88 under the new system. As such it would appear that the men would have more of an area to cover although against this it should be recalled that no lookouts/flagmen were now needed and as such the new system was undoubtedly more efficient in manpower use.

The Advent of the Occupation Key.

So far the system had only been tried on routes where there was one 'staff' section, of limited length and on a line having a fairly restricted train service. As such the scope for economy was dictated by that which could be achieved in this way. It may be accurate to describe the original system as being one of 'telephone maintenance'. What would come next was the introduction of an 'occupation key' allied to an electrical lock. This would be the first of two developments that would revolutionise matters over the next decades.

The actual lock took the form of what was hinted previously and became the Occupation Key Instrument. Three designs of these were evolved. The earliest was a circular instrument (see also top illustration on p44), having in the centre of the front face a key hole and above this a small glass window. Several instruments having the same lock configuration would be wired in series within the section and through which circuit would also pass the current for the release of the single line 'token'. Simply put, if the occupation key was within one of the instruments, a token/staff could not be released for a train. The ganger's instructions were now that he may only have possession of the line when in possession of the occupation key. With the key removed, a token for a train could not be obtained. In service electrical failures were few but when they did occur the train service would also be delayed with pilotman working having to be substituted. Additionally the system could be defeated by unintended simple human error; if a key were lost, misplaced, or as also occurred when the ganger completed his work, removed his trolley and tools from the line and simply forgot to restore the key into an instrument. Fortunately most gangers and men lived near their site of work, so it was not unknown for the signalman to despatch the lad-porter post-haste to the ganger's home. Result, a red-faced ganger and a 'please explain' approach from the local inspector.

In consequence a rapid alteration was a hole being drilled in the face of the key through which a length of chain and hook were added. This change dates from 1908 and is explained in a memorandum on behalf of W.W. Grierson, then Chief Engineer at Paddington:

"Economic Maintenance of Permanent Way, Occupation Key lost at Pembridge 20th May 1908. – A Ganger whilst riding on a velocipede car recently lost an Occupation Key from his pocket, and in consequence a passenger train was seriously delayed. In order to prevent a recurrence of this, Mr. A.T. Blackall is arranging to attach to every Occupation Key a short chain and hook, similar to those attached to the warning whistles, to enable each Ganger to secure his key to his clothing while it is in his possession. Please note, and issue the necessary instructions to your Gangers concerned. Yours truly..."*

K67809/62

PRIVATE & NOT FOR PUBLICATION.

GREAT WESTERN RAILWAY.

(Circular No. 1726.)

Economic System of Permanent Way Maintenance on Single Lines worked under the Electric Train Staff or Electric Train Tablet Regulations.

On Single Lines worked under the Electric Train Staff or Electric Train Tablet Regulations, where the Economic System of Permanent Way Maintenance is in force, the following regulation must in future be strictly observed in connection with every case of occupation granted to the Engineering Department men :—

Whenever a Ganger intimates to the Signalman who has given him permission to obtain an Occupation Key, that the Key has been replaced in the Key Box and ordinary working may be resumed, the Signalmen must immediately withdraw an Electric Train Staff or Electric Train Tablet in accordance with Rule 27 (Testing Instruments) of the Electric Train Staff and Electric Train Tablet Regulations, and the Ganger must remain in the hut until the test has been made and the Signalman has informed him that everything is again in order.

J. MORRIS,
Superintendent of the Line.

W. W. GRIERSON,
Chief Engineer.

PADDINGTON,
May, 1907.

*on the New Radnor branch between Leominster and Titley.

In some cases an even more drastic course of action was taken to limit loss – or forgetfulness - with the chain attached to what was in effect a sizeable cube of wood, similar to the oak keys used to hold the rail in place in a chair. This is thought to have been a local preference. It should also be explained that for the moment we are referring only to single-lines, trolleys of varying sorts were of course used in connection with maintenance on main lines but here the occupation key system was not used. **(There was a solitary exception to this which will be described later.)**

The reliability or otherwise (see photo caption page

This page *- Brass occupation keys from two separate lines. Far left is from the Minehead branch. This line was considered for economic working in 1905 but at the time was rejected although some economy in manpower was achieved. Instead the route went straight to the Motor Economic System in 1932. The second key is from the former Cambrian system between 'Arenig & 11m 55ch'. Note especially the face has been ground and the locations changed from what would have been originally shown. This was a common practice in later years and applied to several routes, gang lengths being altered for a variety of reasons. Although at first glance both keys appear similar, careful examination reveals the configurations to be different. Despite from the later 'Motor' periods, keys from the original economic system with hand trolleys and occupation keys were of identical type.*

Opposite page *- Occupation key and Annett's key combined, for the section from Tavistock to Lydford. The Annett's key allowed the ganger access to unlock the ground frame mid-section serving the Pitts Cleeve Quarry branch.*

56) of the system meant that any failings that did occur would initially be recorded in the appropriate signal box train register, sadly few of these have survived from the GWR system over the years.

The actual occupation key – a piece of brass shaped as a key approximately 8oz in weight and 6in long - would be retained in one of the instruments when not out with the ganger. The electrical equipment used had first been patented by C.M. Jacobs (Patent No 8064 applied for on 7th April 1904 and accepted 2nd May 1905. Further Patents referring to the system were No 424 applied for on 9th January 1905 and accepted 28th September 1905, and No 11460 applied for on 14th May 1909 and accepted on 5th May 1910.) Interestingly the actual equipment was subsequently marketed by Tyer & Co Ltd no doubt under licence.

At this stage it may also be appropriate to afford some brief biographical details as regards certain of the named individuals and commencing with Mr Jacobs. Charles Mark Jacobs had first entered GWR service in what was then the Telegraph Department at Hereford Barton in 1882. He transferred to the chief offices of the same department at Paddington in October 1887 and in August 1896 was appointed Technical Assistant to H.T. Goodenough the then Telegraph Superintendent. Further promotion followed after 1903 with the position of Electrical Assistant to the Signal Engineer - this was after the signal and telegraph departments had been amalgamated. In this role he is also known for the development of electric token and ATC working and eventually rose to become Signal Engineer of the GWR in May 1928. He retired in February 1936.

This first patent, although credited to Jacobs, may well have simply been conveniently annotated in his name. There is indeed some suggestion the actual concept was originally by a lesser mortal within the department, although if this were the case then any due credit was never given.

On the lineside, the possession of the occupation key was a tangible safeguard to the men, for it instilled confidence in the knowledge a train would not approach.

Previously the only guarantee this could not occur was that the signalman would recall the line was in the possession of the ganger and as such human frailty might play a part. With the introduction of the key system responsibility was passed to the driver who knew full well he could not enter a section without the authority of the token – this was impossible to obtain if the occupation key was out of circuit. For a driver to enter a section without a token was also liable to instant dismissal.

Up to now the only lines to have benefited from the scheme were those where the whole line under economic maintenance was worked as a single 'staff' section, although, dependant upon distance several permanent way gangs may have been involved. In practice a ganger having possession of a section may have men from his gang to work at two separate points, still perfectly safe as long as the key remained out of circuit. However on some lines, the 'staff/token' sections were shorter than the designated gang length and on others the gang length might not be as long as the 'staff/token' system.

The solution arrived at by the engineers at Reading was the use of a modified occupation key system and one where further benefits could be achieved. Where a gang had sole responsibility for a section of line between two existing signal boxes there was no change, a single key was provided. If however the section between signal boxes was covered by more than one gang, then it could be that two different sets of instruments would be needed as the gangers' section would butt-up to each other (NEVER overlap) and as such both occupation keys would need to be restored before the 'token' for the train could be released. Obviously the adjoining occupation key sections would also have occupation keys with a different key configuration (but see 'Helston' notes on p57) – this gave rise to the example illustrations opposite where the gangers section clearly ended mid-section rather than at a specific station/ signal-box. The signal boxes at each end of the 'staff' section would still need to co-operate for the release of an occupation key but now this could involve either or both keys being out for work, the section not being able to be restored for the passage of a train until both occupation keys had themselves been restored. Hence enter the era of the 'Occupation Control Instrument'.

This new arrangement foretold of a rapid acceleration in the provision of economic maintenance as routes involving multiple permanent way gangs and 'staff' sections could be included. It is believed the first line to be dealt with in this way was that between Bewdley and Tenbury Wells and which at 13m 76ch also involved three 'staff' sections. This original installation here was brought into use on 5th June 1905 with occupation control instruments added and brought into use on 23rd October 1911 – see overleaf and also the chronological sequence on pages 54/55. The Witney and Fairford route would follow shortly afterwards. (Moving ahead in time the Fairford line is interesting for in 1930 part only, between bampton and the terminus) was converted to Motor Trolley working, presumably the first section from Yarnton to Bampton was similarly adopted later. The accompanying contemporary drawing from the Paddington Record clearly indicates the original boundary north of Neen Sollars. The fact this was altered later did not mean the revised arrangement was unreliable, purely that it was discovered that further economy was still possible.

With the avowed aim of financial advantage as the

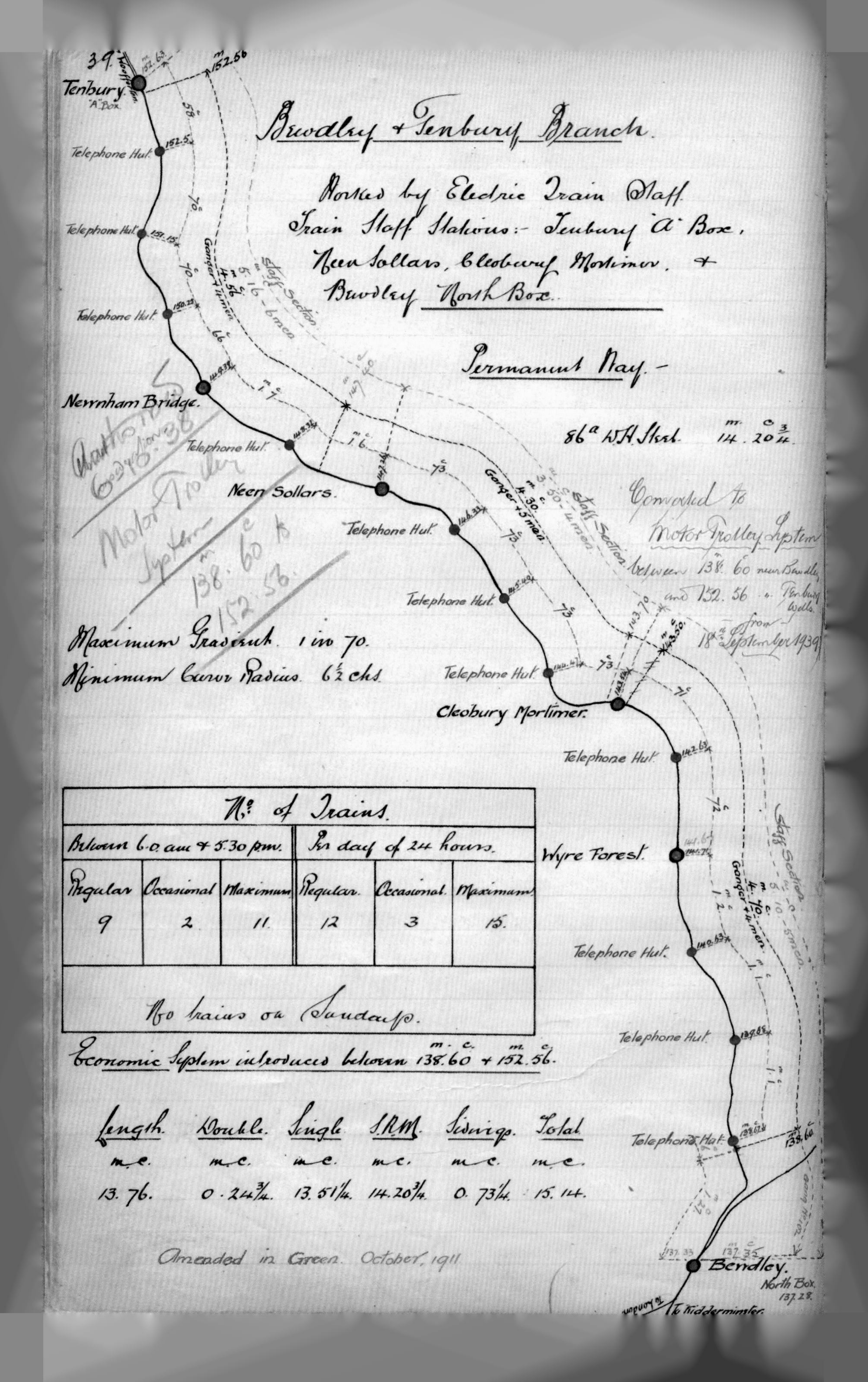

Bewdley & Tenbury Branch.

Worked by Electric Train Staff.
Train Staff Stations:- Tenbury "A" Box, Neen Sollars, Cleobury Mortimer, & Bewdley North Box.

Permanent Way.-

86a W.H. Steel. 14m. 20¾c.

Converted to Motor Trolley System between 138m. 60c near Bewdley and 152. 56 " Tenbury Wells from 18th September 1939.

Maximum Gradient. 1 in 70.
Minimum Curve Radius. 6½ chs.

No. of Trains.					
Between 6.0 am & 5.30 pm.			Per day of 24 hours.		
Regular	Occasional	Maximum	Regular	Occasional	Maximum
9	2	11.	12	3	15.
No trains on Sundays.					

Economic System introduced between 138m. 60c. & 152m. 56c.

Length.	Double.	Single	S.R.M.	Sidings.	Total
m.c.	m.c.	m.c.	m.c.	m.c.	m.c.
13. 76.	0. 24¾.	13. 51¼.	14. 20¾.	0. 73¼.	15. 14.

Amended in Green. October, 1911.

No. of Huts ~~to be~~ provided with Telephones & Occupation Keys }	11
No. of Telephones & Occupation Keys at Stations }	5.
Telephone only at Bewdley - North Box	1.
	17.

~~Actual Cost~~ - Estimated cost of Installation.-

	£.	s.	d
17 Telephones, and 16 Occupation key Instruments,	265.	0.	0
11 Huts + 3 Watches.	61.	3.	0
1 Velocipede Car. 3 Mechanical Trollies.	43.	15.	0
Total	£ 369.	18.	0

Under Standard Rules the Branch was maintained by.-

	Total No. of men.	Wages per annum.	No. of men per mile
4. Gangs of 5 men each.-	20.	965. 9. 4.	1.32.

Under new System.-

1 Gang of 6 men, + 2 Gangs of 5 men each. } Additional man taken on in Gang No. 64. 14/8/11	16 ~~15~~ ~~16.~~	724. 2. 0 ~~768. 6. 0.~~	.99 ~~1.05~~
Gross saving in men + wages per ann:	4 ~~5~~ ~~4.~~	241. 7. 4. ~~197. 3. 4~~	.33. ~~.27.~~

* Further saving of 1 man. Nov. 1906. when 2 add.l velocipede Cars were supplied -

[illegible] Jan/09

The Ganger at Cleobury Mortimer Station inspects the whole Branch once daily on a Velocipede Inspection Car. Each Ganger to be provided with a Watch, also a Mechanical Trolley so that men may readily pass from one part of the length to another.

Economic system brought into operation 5th June, 1905.

2 Add.l Velocipede Cars ordered for this Branch - 15.9.05

* A further saving of 1 man effected in November, 1906 by slightly re-arranging the lengths as corrected in red, + supplying each Ganger with a Velocipede Car to inspect his own length daily.

Economic System brought into operation 23rd October, 1911.

Installation of Telephone / Economic System of Maintenance - not all confirmed as subsequently converted to include key instruments.									
Route / Branch	**Route Length (maintained length in brackets)**	**Introduction of system**	**Type of rail originally provided**	**Number of telephones**	**Minimum radius curve (chains)**	**Maximum Gradient 1 in**	**Cost**	**Estimated Original Saving per annum**	**Note**
Helston	8m 76 ch (9m 78 ch)	30-5-1904	86lbs in chairs	11	12	60	£355 17s 10d	£149.10	Converted to 'motor' 28-4-1930
Yealmpton	6m 44ch (8m 15ch)	1-7-1904	68lbs in chairs	8	15	60	£236 3s 8d	£105 6s	Converted to 'modified' motor 12-10-1931
Abbotsbury	6m 8ch (7m 60ch)	18-3-1905	Vignole	9	12	44	£49 4s 6d	£62 8s	
Shipston-on-Stour	9m 7ch (9m 60ch)	1-5-1905	Bullhead and flange	12	7	53	£288 8s 3d	£143	Converted to 'modified' motor 28-9-1931
Madeley	3m 58ch (4m 28.75ch)	5-6-1905	Bullhead	5	16	64	£82 18s 4d	£44 4s	Converted to motor 5-10-1931
Malmesbury	6m 46ch (7m 16ch)	29-5-1905	Bullhead and vignole	9	10	66	£64 5s 9d	£62 8s	See notes in text.
Bewdley and Tenbury Wells	13m 76ch (15m 14ch)	5-6-1905	Bullhead	17	6.5	70	£369 18s	£197 3s 4d	See notes in text.
Witney & Fairford	21m 74 (25m 70.5ch)	5-6-1905	Bullhead	17	20	100	£450	£230.2s	Converted to motor 6-1-1930
Presteign	5m 54ch (6m 8 ch)	6-11-1905	Bullhead and vignole	8	16	43	£113 6s	£42 18s	
Alcester	6m 40ch (6m 78ch)	1-1-1906	Bullhead	9	9	66	£200 16s	£105 6s	
Leominster & Bromyard	20m 68ch (27m)	5-3-1906	Bullhead	29	10	50	£560 5s	£228 16s	See notes in text. Converted to motor 30-12 1929
Much Wenlock	17m 12ch (21m 32ch)	14-5-1906	Mainly Bullhead	23	13	40	£463 4s	£305 18s 8d	Mostly converted to motor 14-9-1931
Highworth	5m 39.25ch (6m 9.5ch)	2-7-1906	Bullhead and vignole	10	10	44	£62 16s	£106 12s	
Ketley	4m 41c (6m 31.5ch)	4-6-1906	Bullhead?	6	9.5	40	£115 16s	£65	Converted to Motor 5-10-1931
Eardisley	6m 63ch (7m 12.75ch)	29-10-1906	Bullhead and vignole	10	8	44	£271 16s	£149 10s	
Kington & New Radnor	6m 46.5ch (7m 44.25ch)	29-10-1906	Bullhead	10	6	50	£257 16s	£85 16s	
Bala Junction & Dolgelley	18m 41.5ch (20m 76.25ch)	17.12.1906	Bullhead?	23	8	50	£458	£262 12	Extended 15-4-1929 Converted to Motor 9-4-1934

Watlington	8m 55ch (9m 58.5ch)	3-1-1907	Bullhead and 38ch of Vignole	11	13	60	£103 9s 11d		See notes in text
Kingsbridge	12m 23ch (14m 16ch)	14-1-1907	Bullhead	16	12	50	£272 10s	£210 12s	
Cirencester	3m 75.5ch (4m 73ch)	4-2-1907	Mainly Bullhead	6	10.5	264	£103 4s 11d	£46 16s	
Tetbury	7m 4.5ch (7m 69ch)	4-2-1907	Mainly Vignole	11	10.5	66	£171 2s 3d	£107 18s	Converted to Motor 17-10-1932
St. Ives	4m 26ch (5m 78ch)	11-3-1907	Bullhead	8	12	60	£154 6s 7d	£106 12s	
Moretonhampstead	12m 9ch (13m 59ch)	29-4-1907	Bullhead	16	10	49	£334	£210 12s	
Lostwithiel & Fowey	4m 20ch	7-5-1907	Bullhead	8	7	80	£126 1s	£44 4s	
Severn Valley Line	28m 22ch (35m 61.5ch)	23-9-1907	Bullhead	37	16	100	£767 8s 9d	£312	Partly converted to Motor – see text
Ross to Little Mill Junction	29m 47.25ch (34m 67ch)	7-10-1907	Mainly Bullhead	39	8.5	100	£618 7s 5d	£325	Converted to Motor 2-2-1931
Wye Valley Branch	13m 9ch (14m 54ch)	6-1-1908	Mainly Bullhead also flange	18	19	66	£263	£218 8s	Converted to Motor 17-8-1931
Boncarth to Cardigan	6m 44ch (7m 29ch)	31-8-1908	Mainly flange	10	8	35	£157 14s	£57 4s	See notes in text – later Motor
Pencader to Newcastle Emlyn	10m 2.5ch (12m 37.5ch)	14-9-1908	Mainly Bullhead	14	9	58	£294	£101 8s	Converted to Motor 10-6-1929
Marlborough Branch	5m 33ch (5m 63.5ch)	1-8-1910	Mainly bridge with some bullhead	7	15	58	£122	£109 4s	
Launceston Branch	18m 47ch (20m 78ch)	26-12-1910	Not stated	26	15	55	£602 10s	£237 18s	Converted to Motor 6-2-1933
Bridport	11m 21ch (12m 78.75ch)	5-6-1911	Mainly flange also bullhead	15	7	50	£384	£157 6s	
Chard	13m 3ch (16m 39.25ch)	17-6-1912	Mainly Bullhead	18	17	79	£565 10s	£237 18s	Converted to 'modified' Motor 27-7-1931
Barnstaple Branch (part)	23m 65ch (28m 75.75ch)	30-9-1912	Bullhead	33	12	58	£722 5s	£301 12S	Converted to Motor 11-9-1933
Lampeter & Aberayron	12m 10ch (13m 10.75ch)	11-11-1912	Mainly flange	9	Not stated	40	£262 10s	£96 4s	Converted to Motor 8-8-1932
Lambourn	11m 70.5ch (13m 15.5ch)	1-9-1913?	Not stated	17	Not stated	Not stated	£398	£98 16s	See notes in text

Unfortunately, any comments or reports over the reliability or otherwise of the original occupation-key system are not recorded in any GWR records located. The basic system also had its limitations. On a section of line between two signal boxes but which was divided for maintenance between two gangs (and consequently with one key each), understandably only one key could be removed at any one time. Additionally if a fault were to develop in any of the key instruments then this would also mean the token system was similarly out of order. To deal with the eventuality of equipment failure but where a signal section corresponded with a ganger's section, the GWR introduced the Occupation Control instrument, see top left. This contained two slides and was operated as follows: upon receiving a request for the occupation key to be removed either from the instrument within the signal box or if the key had been left in an intermediate instrument, the signalman would first confer with his signalman colleague at the other end of the section. Assuming permission is given, the man at the opposite end will hold-down his ringing key on the token instrument. This then allows the 'Control' slide on the left to be pulled fully out. This in turn releases the slide on the right which when pulled fully out sends a release to the relevant key box allowing the occupation key to be withdrawn. The slides cannot be returned to their normal position until the occupation key has been restored in the instrument. Only then will the line also be restored and a conventional token be able to be obtained for a train. There was also a three slide control instrument operated in similar fashion with one control slide and two 'B' slides. This was used in similar form but applied when two gangers sections, each with their own key, met mid-section between signal boxes. One or both occupation keys could thus be released but naturally each could only be restored to an instrument within their appropriate group - naturally the keys would have different end configurations to correspond with the appropriate key-way on the instrument. Only when both keys had been restored might the railway be given up for the passage of a train. The control instruments were painted red, lined out on the sides with black and had a polished wooden top. The 'tombstone' key instruments were black on the face, base and rear with red for the casing - this shows up as the lighter colour in the b/w images. Token instruments were painted in similar style. In the view right (location not recorded) a single line key token, 2-slide control instrument and a 'tombstone' occupation key instrument may be seen. Note also the engraved ivorine ring on the control instrument indicating the section to which it refers, in this case it is 'Stow on the Wold to Kingham West.'

rationale for the expansion of the economic system of maintenance it is interesting to recollect also that to some extent the needs of the workforce were not totally forgotten as per two memoranda from Paddington in 1906. The first was of 23rd April, and referred to:

"Economic Maintenance of Permanent Way. Oilskins for Gangers using Velocipede Cars. – In further reference to this matter (- no earlier correspondence has been located): after consideration it has been decided that each Ganger who is required to ride on a velocipede car, on a Branch where the Economic System is in operation, shall be supplied with an oilskin coat, leggings and Sou' Wester hat.
It must, however, be clearly understood that this special concession is made only to Gangers who have to carry out the daily inspection of their lengths on velocipede cars, on account of the different conditions under which they work and the greater exposure to which they are subjected in wet weather.
Please acknowledge receipt: and send forward a requisition for such garments for each of your Gangers concerned.
Yours truly…"

Further correspondence evidently ensued with the following noted for 8th October 1906:

"Oilskins for Gangers using Velocipede Cars. – As the result of the enquiry made by my letter of the 12th ultimo: it has been decided that oilskin coats reaching to a little above the men's knees would be the most suitable and result in the least inconvenience when they are working the velocipede cars, as the leggings to be supplied will reach to the top of the thighs.
I enclose the requisitions which you sent forward, and shall be glad if you will have them amended as may be necessary returning them to me as soon as possible.
Mr Stanier informs me that the average length of coats to reach a little above the knees would be as follows, according to the height of each man concerned, viz:

Height	*Length of Coat*	
5' 4"	*37 inches long*	
5' 6"	*38*	*do*
5' 8"	*39*	*do*
5' 10"	*40*	*do*
6' 0"	*41½*	*do*
6' 2"	*42½*	*do*

Yours truly…"

Expansion of the System

Chronologically we now need to return to 1904 at this stage, for having described the concept and operational advantage of having occupation key instruments as well as telephones, it should be mentioned that the first line on which these were installed was the 8m 76 ch Helston branch from Gwinear Road and which were brought into use on 30th May 1904. Economy was achieved here with a total of nine men in two gangs compared with the previous three gangs and twelve men. Eleven telephones were provided and with the total cost referred to as £355 17s 10d and which could be broken down as £275 for the apparatus, £20 for the two velocipedes, £22 10s for two mechanical trolleys and £4 2s for two watches. The saving in wages was put at £149 10s and meaning the installation would pay for itself in less than two years.

The Paddington Record refers to the branch at that time as having just the one staff section although there is a pencil note "Nancegollen Loop" followed by a question mark. The original description of the operation the branch from the source material is also of interest, "There are two groups of Occupation Key Instruments – one group for each gang. One key is provided for each group, and may be used in any box in that group. If the key belonging to one group of instruments is inserted in a key box belonging to the other group the normal working cannot be restored". A further pencil note accompanied this paragraph, "This does not agree with the Instructions for working the Branch included on Page 102 of Appendix to No 6 Service Time Table". Unfortunately a copy of the Appendix referred to has not been located.

Perhaps even more important is the impression that a key could be inserted in that belonging to another group. If that were the case it was surely quickly modified to have a different configuration. It should be mentioned also that there had been a signal box at Nancegollen since 1887 but it is believed to have operated only as a ground frame until 1908. In any event the boundary between the two gangs was 49 chains north of Nancegollen. No date is given in the Paddington Record for the insertion of the pencil notes referred to.

Helston may very well then have been unique and what can now be seen to be the shortcomings of working were very quickly apparent. Interestingly rarely within the Paddington Record is there ever any reference to modifications to the system and likewise no record of such changes has been located in Minute Books and records elsewhere.

Two other points may also be mentioned, the first is in relation to the choice of Helston for what was in effect a pioneering installation – a hand written note in red in the record does indeed refer to it being the first branch to be equipped with Occupation Key Instruments, but why choose Helston? Surely it is a little strange that the first branch to be so equipped was almost 300 miles from the Signal Works at Reading and so could hardly be said to be within ease of travelling for the engineers on what was a totally new and untried system. Indeed later pioneering experiments involving signalling, viz ATC, Electric Power Frames, Intermediate Signals, Route Setting etc, were all undertaken within the London Division. Secondly there is no record of the use of Occupation Key Instruments on what were passenger carrying lines being inspected by the Board of Trade and who would otherwise certainly verify all new signalling and track alterations on such routes. The National Achive (Public Record Office) 'MT6' files seemingly empty of such references, although it is unlikely that they never existed, more like, they have not been located or no longer survive.

In the same way that drivers and guards of loose-fitted freight trains were expected to exercise caution when descending gradients, so gangers were similarly advised. This type of notice is an example which would have been seen on several lines - this particular one is believed to have been in the Forest of Dean. The criteria referred to was that caution should be exercised when descending any gradient steeper than 1 in 80. A trolley used on gradients of this type must also be fitted with brakes - "...in working order...".

Next to be operated under the system was the Yealmpton branch which commenced the new regime from 1st July 1904. Statistical information on the branch is given in the table but it may be interesting to work out that by this time the cost of each individual telephone could be stated to be in the order of £5 each whilst the Occupation Key Instruments were costed at just under £24 each. This was at a time when the lowest grade packer on the Permanent Way staff would be earning little more than £1 per week.

A study of the information in the Paddington Record reveals that from now on the equipment installed and type of installation also varied considerably. Cheapest of all were those where a single gang was involved and which meant that only telephones were provided. This was the case with the Abbotsbury branch where two gangs totalling eight men were combined into a single gang of seven. The cost quoted for the installation of nine telephones, five huts, and provision of velocipede and trolley was just £49 4s 6d. For this amount there is no way instruments could have been provided, although this does appear to be retrograde step. The Abbotsbury branch commenced operation under the new arrangements from 18th March 1905.

Next in order of date was the Moreton & Shipston branch. This dead-end line was unusual in that up to that time there had been no means of communication along the line and the provision of telephones was also then of use to the traffic department. The cost of £221 5s 5d referred to 12 telephones and also poles and wires. It is unlikely then that any instruments were provided and whilst this was economy in its most basic sense it still allowed for a saving of three men with nine now employed in two gangs instead of the previous 12 in three. Interestingly one of the nine men was retained especially to maintain the four miles of horse tramway which led off the branch at Longdon Road. Originally only one inspection car was provided but there were two mechanical trolleys. A second inspection car was added from 29th October 1906.

Despite the fact that only telephones were provided, this was perfectly safe provided the rules appertaining to advising occupation to the signalman were complied with (as per the Golden Valley line etc.). Unfortunately this does not appear to have been the case on the Shipstone branch in 1930 and which although chronologically out of sequence is worthy of inclusion at this stage. The Shipstone accident (previously described on p45) is the only known accident to a ganger whilst on a velocipede although unfortunately with fatal consequences.

Another Midlands area branch dealt with in 1905 was that from Madeley Junction to Lightmoor Junction. This section was just three miles fifty-eight chains long but the saving of one man in the single gang involved was considered sufficient to warrant the expense of installing telephones and occupation key instruments.

The original Malmesbury branch from Dauntsey to the terminus was the first in Wiltshire to be equipped and brought into use on 29th May 1905. Mike Fenton in his erudite history of the Malmesbury Branch (published by Wild Swan), refers to authorisation having been given previously in minutes dating from August 1903 and it is very likely then that a number of the installations described in this work were approved either individually or under a blanket approval from about that time onwards. Interestingly, despite the fact that nine telephones were required, only six were installed, use being made of three existing telephones located at Dauntsey, Great Somerford, and Malmesbury. Special instructions also applied to this line from the local Divisional Engineer in that the ganger was also required to walk the track on occasions. Why this should have been specifically mentioned is not reported.

The new Malmesbury installation allowed for one gang of seven men to be in charge compared with the previous two gangs each of four men. Later on, maintenance on the branch was altered considerably from Monday 17th July 1933 in consequence of the abandonment of the section south to Dauntsey and the revised branch connection with the Badminton line at Little Somerford. At this time the original branch gang was disbanded and responsibility for maintenance passed to Gang No 63 whose area also covered the main line. It was stated that "...a mechanical trolley was still employed...", but it is not certain if this generalisation also implied that the velocipede and occupation keys were likewise retained. Further statistical information on the Malmesbury installation is in the table.

The Bewdley to Tenbury Wells installation has of course been mentioned previously – the first line on which control instruments were used. This was also by far the most ambitious scheme to date and which although at 13 miles 76 chains was slightly shorter than the Golden Valley route, the Worcester scheme did involve three separate gangs. For the first time also one Ganger, that from Cleobury Mortimer, was given responsibility for inspecting the whole branch once daily, which, with a maximum gradient of 1 in 70 and considering the round trip distance of some 28 miles, would probably have occupied a fair amount of time every day. Clearly, though authority were quick enough to recognise that such a task was impractical as in November 1906, it was agreed to provide each of the three gangers with a velocipede car. This change though took some time to materialise as it was not until 15th September 1907 that the new vehicles arrived.

As also referred to the Paddington Record does not appear necessarily to record all alterations to the installations over the years, although in so far as the Bewdley to Tenbury Wells route is concerned, there are some additional interesting snippets. The first was in November 1906 when a minor readjustment of the lengths allowed for the saving of one further man.

One final entry on the pages appertaining to this route – and in a slightly different pen, simply states, "Economic System brought into operation 23rd October 1911", and which is of course at odds with the original date six and a half years earlier. For the reasons given earlier this may well have been the date control instruments were installed, a feasible assumption based on the date of the final patent. The Bewdley to Tenbury Wells route was later converted to motor trolley operation and which was itself brought into use on 18th September 1939.

Two other installations were completed in 1905, the first the Witney and Fairford branch from Yarnton Junction and which was by far the longest geographically at 21 miles 74 chains. Similar economy was achieved here as with Bewdley to Tenbury Wells, four gangs of six men each replacing seven gangs of four. Indeed when it is considered that under previous arrangements two men from each gang would have been required for look-out work, it would appear that considerable advantage was achieved not just in financial terms but also in efficiency. Also as with the Bewdley - Tenbury Wells scheme, the original arrangement had been for one ganger only to inspect the complete route daily 'Sundays included', on a single 'light velocipede car'. Even allowing for the easier gradients on the Fairford branch compared with those to Tenbury Wells, this was quickly found to be an economy too far and three additional cars were provided, one for each ganger, from 1st January 1906.

Again dealing with the Fairford story, and from a penned note dated 13th December 1941, it does not appear that control instruments were installed until that year, the justification for this being the quote, "The Signal department are carrying out alterations to the signalling between Yarnton Junction and Bampton and will take the opportunity of improving the Occupation Key arrangements so as to give Gangs 150 / 151 simultaneous occupation of the Eynsham-Witney section. It was stated by the P.Way Inspector that the Mechanical Trolleys were still in operation and the O.K.System was used very extensively". Conversely it must also be pointed out that both the Tenbury and Fairford installations involved a similar amount of equipment, that for Tenbury "17 telephones and 16 occupation key instruments", cost of £265, and for Fairford, "17 telephones and occupation key instruments" – the number of instruments not specified although likely to have been 17. The cost though in this case was reported as £350.

The final line to be equipped at this time was the little Presteign branch from Titley on the line between New

A mid-section 'box' the contents of which can just be discerned and include a telephone and occupation key instrument, the location is not given. Behind is the telegraph pole from which the various circuit wires would be taken into the box - notice the telegraph insulator on the left. This hut has a door that opens outwards, others moved up/down, as per the view opposite. Interestingly the telephone has an obvious mouthpiece but where did the ganger speak into?

Radnor and Leominster. At just 5 miles 54 chains just one gang of five men had been involved but with an additional man on permanent secondment from neighbouring gang No 84. The new arrangement allowed for the use of just five men. Two interesting notes appertaining to the line at this time, the first that the branch was not inspected by the ganger on Sundays – the justification for this being there were no Sunday trains, and secondly a saving on the cost of providing a velocipede car on the basis that, "The Divisional Engineer has a spare..." – which was obviously then transferred for use on the line.

The years from 1906 through to 1913

Installations were destined to continue apace in 1906 – and beyond, no doubt based upon the advantages gained. It would have been reasonable to assume that some paperwork would have existed at some stage in the form of Divisional Engineers reports on the success of or any difficulties encountered, but again any such files have not been located.

Nine lines were equipped in 1906. The first brought into use on 1st January – so clearly work on this would have been undertaken the previous year, was the Alcester Branch running between Alcester and Bearley and which was now maintained by a single gang of six men compared with the previous two gangs of four. The system continued in operation on the line until about 1939/40 when the following note appeared, "Since the outbreak of war this gang has been split up – the Ganger alone being left to look after the length. The branch has been closed to traffic and the line used for storage purposes. No use can be made of the velocipede car or mechanical trolley and the Gang has been reduced to Ganger, Sub-Ganger and 1 Lengthman" – dated 20th March 1940. The 1940 comments are interesting in that here would appear to be proof that on routes where the later motor-economic system was not installed the original equipment of 1904 type velocipedes and pump

A trolley run-off point. Short sections of rail set at 90° to the running line were commonplace in the days of both the economic and later the motor-economic eras. As referred to in the caption for the illustration opposite, a 'box' containing a telephone and instrument is on the left. In order to manoeuvre a trolley on to the rails a small turntable might be carried (common in the days of motor trolley working) alternatively the trolley might be physically manhandled by the men. Note the run-off slopes away from the running line. *Austin Attewell*

trolleys were otherwise still in use.

Next came the Leominster and Bromyard branch brought into use on Monday 3rd March 1906 – approval had been given by the Engineering Committee on 3rd August previous. (A pencil note mentions the Divisional Superintendent's Notice as to the commencement of operation being 13th July 1908. In every other respect entries within the Paddington Record are totally chronological and in consequence 1906 is used in this work.) As with the entry on Presteign in the previous chapter no costing was given for a velocipede as again the Divisional Engineer had a spare. Clearly also the lessons of the distance any one ganger could reasonably be expected to traverse on inspection had been learnt, for the new arrangement of four gangs saw the comment that, "Each ganger has been provided with a watch and inspects his own length daily (Sundays excepted) upon a Velocipede Inspection Car. A Mechanical Trolley has been provided for each man".

But even this simple statement raises questions. The finances clearly refer to four mechanical trolleys yet the addenda mentions the engineer providing the velocipede and with the note mentioning each ganger inspecting daily. Does this then mean they shared the velocipede? Probably unlikely, but what other conclusion is there from the available evidence?

Another Midlands branch was dealt with next, the Much Wenlock line, and which had the following note appended to the information for the route, "This line was worked by Electric Train Staff between Buildwas Junction and Much Wenlock, and by Train Staff and Ticket with auxiliary Block Telegraph between Much Wenlock and Marsh Farm Junction. Electric Train Staff working installed throughout, at an estimated cost of £400, to enable Economic System to be introduced…". This installation saw the original workforce of five gangs of five men in each reduced to three gangs totalling 17 men, and with two of those displaced from the branch transferred to the Buildwas Gang No 110. In the audit of equipment provided the number of Inspections Cars, Mechanical Trolleys and watches would then have been expected to have been three of each, but in all cases 'four' is written down but without further comment. The line was incorporated into the new system from 14th May 1906.

Some years later on 6th March 1922, a further note refers specifically to Gang No 75 based at Much Wenlock and which consisted of six men who were responsible for a distance of 5 miles and 70 chains. It was stated that, "Use is not made of the mechanical trolley on the length owing to the severe gradients. The car will probably be used on the Division, and the Ganger's watch is required, as the occupation key is used when trolleying stores etc. Ganger's overalls will be withdrawn". Clearly then the original principals still applied and gives confirmation to the belief that the Permanent Way staff were some of the toughest breed working for the railway. An extra point to make at this stage is that it has been suggested that certain branch lines were not selected for conversion to the system due to the gradients involved and this may indeed have been the case in later years as experience was gained. Certainly the Much Wenlock and Ketley branches – see next entry, shared a common maximum gradient of 1 in 40 although there is no record of difficulties with use of the mechanical trolley on this latter line, notwithstanding the fact that the section under occupation was 5 miles 70 chains compared with 4 miles 41 chains.

The Ketley branch between Ketley station and Lightmoor Junction came next on 4th June 1906, and with the installation details making particular comment that the short section from Ketley station to Ketley Junction was not included. Over a distance of just a fraction more than 4½ miles there was limited scope for economy, but this was achieved through the amalgamation of two gangs totalling seven men into one of six and so proving that the GWR was intent on the pursuit of saving even when just one man was involved. The saving quoted, £65 per annum, would tend to imply that one of the previous Gangers posts was superfluous, but as before the fate of the man concerned is not reported. The record is also not completely clear whether the short section from Lightmoor Junction to Madeley was also under maintenance. Probably unlikely as a key box is only shown at Lightmoor Junction and not at Madeley and may then refer to the gang having responsibility for this section even if it did not come under the modified form of working.

The short branch from Highworth Junction near Swindon to Highworth came next and although recorded at this stage in this work in the Paddington Record it is out of sequence after Kington and New Radnor – **see later**, despite the note that the Economic System was brought into use on 2nd July 1906. This branch saw its permanent way workforce now concentrated in a single gang of six men thus saving two posts although in both cases it was noted an extra man was temporarily employed until the existing vignole rail was re-laid. The cost for the equipment is also interesting being quoted at just £15 for six telephones yet the information also clearly stated that 10 were provided, six in huts and a further four at the stations. The low cost figures quoted cannot necessarily be explained but it is possible only telephones were provided and not occupation key instruments as it is known the branch was worked by a train staff and only one engine in steam until 29th November 1940 when electric token working was substituted. At this late stage it is perhaps unlikely occupation key instruments were then provided.

We now return again to the Midlands area branches, as the next in 1906 was the Eardisley line from the station of that name to Titley. As with the Shipston-on-Stour line, there had previously been no telegraph poles or wires and as these were provided in connection with the operation, the Traffic Department was reported as also benefiting. Special arrangements were also made for the Crossing Keeper at Almeley Crossing to have use of the telephone in the hut there. The date of commencement was 29th October 1906.

This branch also recorded the first reference to the provision of a "Velocipede Car Hut". Priced at £3 it was no doubt of rudimentary construction. All subsequent installations included this feature. The system is believed to have remained in use until the branch was removed in October 1940 but may well have witnessed a modification in the method of operation before this, for it as noted in pencil that a 'Traffic Notice' was issued in February 1927 although its content is not reported.

On the same date as Eardisley commenced the new type of working, the system was also brought into use on two other lines, the first of these being that from Kington Junction (Leominster) though to Kington and which of course had a junction with the previously described Eardisley line at Titley. Similarly the final line to be brought into the economic system of maintenance was that between Kington and New Radnor and it no doubt made practical sense then for the installations to proceed simultaneously on all three lines.

The six and one-half mile Kington to New Radnor route was another which did not have telegraph poles or wires and the installation of these for the Engineering Department was also subsequently used by the Traffic Department. The Paddington Record is also very clear in the means of operation, "Worked by one engine in steam between Kington and New Radnor", which is also mentioned by Nicholas de Courtais in his book *The New Radnor Branch* – published 1992. The staff type was wooden, triangular in section, and painted green. Just one gang of six men would now maintain the branch and which was a saving of two individuals. The cost was quoted as £257 16s, which included a single velocipede and mechanical trolley.

A drawing within the 'New Radnor Branch' book also describes the system but not as per the Paddington Record, and it may well be then that it was modified at some stage although the Paddington Record only contains entries for 1906 with nothing subsequently mentioned. The 1992 branch history includes a drawing of what is a four-handled control instrument (- this may well have been unique as

From the Swindon Stores catalogue (undated): " Trollies - 4 wheel platelayers, 18in diameter on treads." Notice the rudimentary method of braking. Later versions were fitted with pressed steel disc wheels.

previously only two-and-three handled instruments were known of), but again the question is asked, when was this installed? The only conclusion must be subsequent to 1905. Supporting this latter statement is the reference that in 1905 the new arrangement allowed a single gang to maintain the route, whilst the 1992 history refers to one gang overlapping Kington itself from just east of Titley and having responsibility as far as 14 miles 70 chains. A second gang then looked after the branch between 14 miles 70 chains and the terminus at New Radnor.

This then must have been a revision at a date not reported and which no doubt came about consequent upon the introduction of control instruments – and as stated previously probably from 1911 onwards. Further credence to this is in the costings, £210 for 10 telephone huts which is similar to the average of £5 for a telephone and around £5-6 as the cost of each occupation key instrument.

Again according to the 1992 history, the GWR 1925 review into branch line operating costs conceded that £20 per year could be saved on the New Radnor branch by reverting to a wooden train staff – possibly still with gangers occupation but probably based on the simplest telephone system. Certainly a wooden staff was produced at Reading Signal Works but any change to permanent way maintenance at the same time is not recorded.

The area which would later see the greatest concentration of 'occupation key' working on the GWR was on much of the former Cambrian system although most of this would be some years later when the motor economic system was introduced. Prior to 1923 the GWRs inroads into the area of Central Wales were limited, with the line between Bala Junction and Dolgelley selected as the first line in the area to be equipped. At this time the route, although of single track, was reported as being worked by double line disc block telegraph and electric train staff. The accounts reveal the usual costings although the entry for four suits of oilskins was written but then struck though. The new

PRIVATE & NOT FOR PUBLICATION. K 67809/62

GREAT WESTERN RAILWAY.

(Circular No. 1726.)

Economic System of Permanent Way Maintenance on Single Lines worked under the Electric Train Staff or Electric Train Tablet Regulations.

On Single Lines worked under the Electric Train Staff or Electric Train Tablet Regulations, where the Economic System of Permanent Way Maintenance is in force, the following regulation must in future be strictly observed in connection with every case of occupation granted to the Engineering Department men :—

Whenever a Ganger intimates to the Signalman who has given him permission to obtain an Occupation Key, that the Key has been replaced in the Key Box and ordinary working may be resumed, the Signalmen must immediately withdraw an Electric Train Staff or Electric Train Tablet in accordance with Rule 27 (Testing Instruments) of the Electric Train Staff and Electric Train Tablet Regulations, and the Ganger must remain in the hut until the test has been made and the Signalman has informed him that everything is again in order.

J. MORRIS,
Superintendent of the Line.

W. W. GRIERSON,
Chief Engineer.

PADDINGTON,
May, 1907.

As an aside, trolleys were not of course restricted to use on branch lines whilst the basic trolley had also been in use for many years beforehand. This is an 1894 view of men on a trolley, probably inspecting the permanent-way during flooding near Abingdon Road bridge, Oxford in November 1894. The sticks being used by the men would appear to be serving a dual purpose: propulsion of the trolley and also checking the depth of water/ integrity of the permanent way. It is likely the man stood with the bowler hat is the divisional engineer.

arrangement allowed for four gangs of five men in each to maintain the line but as there were only three electric train staff sections at the time boundary cross-overs obviously occurred. The new arrangements commenced on 17th December 1906.

Just beyond Dolgelley was the start of Cambrian Railway metals and it is worth mentioning that the system on the original section from Bala Junction was extended past Dolgelley to Barmouth Junction in April 1929. As with Highworth, and Watlington described next, this line is also out of sequence in the Paddington Register, one possible explanation being the entries were made as work was authorised / commenced and it would be expected then that they would be completed in the same order. Any delay would of course result in such a sequence of recording.

Nearer to Reading was the Watlington branch from Princes Risborough which from the recorded installation cost of the "apparatus", at £35 11s 2d for 11 telephones would imply that no key instruments were provided. The work had been authorised in March 1906 with the line worked by a single train staff with one engine in steam. It was stated the "Economic System was brought into operation 3rd January 1907".

This would certainly appear to be borne out as the

inventory details the usual equipment costs – minus oilskins at this stage, but with the heading "apparatus" mentioned above, written in pencil as if at the time the entries were first made it had not been decided if telephones and instruments would be provided. The present manning arrangement of two gangs of four was referred to with the new system also requiring the same number after which came the following note, "Strength recently reduced by 1 man, and 2 gangs formed instead of 3. One Ganger saved, wages £64 2s per annum. As lengths are long (4m 40ch and 4m 15ch) respectively, it is considered desirable to introduce the economic system". In this case there would appear to have been limited manpower savings and instead a more efficient operation.

A later pencil note dated 'February 1933', stated, "Gangs rearranged and worked under 'Patrolman' system but the cars and trolleys were retained at Mr. Kirkpatrick's request." Another entry states the 'Patrolman' system had been introduced on 26th March 1934. This though would seem to be contradicted by the next entry, this time of 28th April 1939, which commented, "Mr. Kirkpatrick reported in February 1939 that the mechanical Trolleys from this Branch were sent to Swindon about six years ago. The redundant velocipede cars were accordingly sent to Swindon and eventually reconditioned and sent to Gloucester Division. Supt. of the Line was advised that the Mechanical Trolley system would be abandoned and ordinary (Patrolman) maintenance restored". It would certainly seem that in later years men on certain branches, of which Watlington was one, did not utilise the inspection and mechanical trolleys to advantage. A quote from *Country Branch Line Volume 1,* notes, "A pump trolley was kept at Aston Rowant but it was only used on Good Fridays", whilst another quote from the same book notes, "...We had a pump trolley but I don't remember it being used much...".

Devon saw the second installation of 1907, brought into use on 14th January, involving the Kingsbridge branch from Brent. Sixteen telephones were provided with the branch now split into two gangs each of six men compared with four of four. Two electric train staff sections were used to control operation on the line, the first from Brent to Gara Bridge and thence from Gara Bridge to Kingsbridge. This did not exactly coincide with the revised gang boundaries which overlapped at Gara Bridge. The new maintenance came into being on 14th January with the Paddington record also noting for the first time a cost for two suits of oilskins for the gangers at a cost of £1 10s for both. This branch would have control instruments later provided (2-slide type) and the gang lengths altered to coincide with the electric token sections.

Two adjacent branch lines in Gloucestershire came next, the Cirencester and Tetbury lines, both emanating from a junction with the Swindon to Gloucester route at Kemble. Each were equipped and brought into the scheme on the same date, 4th February 1907. Dealing with Cirencester first, a note in the Paddington Record states, "Previously worked by Train Staff & Ticket & Block Telegraph. To enable Economic System to be introduced, Electric Train Staff working was introduced at a cost (estimated) of £100". In so far as the provision of the telephones was concerned, six were installed, four in huts, and two, "At stations or Signal Boxes". This particular phrase appears often throughout the Paddington Register sometimes the word "...or...",also being substituted with, "...and...". From this it may be taken to mean that on certain lines the single line "staff / token" equipment may well have been located within the station buildings – usually the booking office, where it's use could allegedly be supervised by the incumbent Station Master. This arrangement continued until around 1940 on some lines. In other cases changes over the years saw the instruments grouped collectively in the signal box. At main junction stations, Kemble a classic example, the instruments would have been in the signal box from the outset. The Cirencester installation witnessed a saving of one man in the single gang that maintained the branch.

The Tetbury branch was a very similar installation to that described above and also saw the replacement of identical earlier train working by the electric train staff, this time at an estimated cost of £95. One gang of seven men was now substituting for the previous arrangement of two gangs totally nine men.

Remaining in the West Country, but further west still was the St. Ives branch, just 4 miles 26 chains in length. Although recorded as equipped and operating from 11th March 1907, it was later reported, on 20th November 1934, that, "The Economic System has been abandoned here for several years" – there is then a reference to a bundle of correspondence, '67809/58'. A clue as to the reason for the system being unused may be gauged from the record of trains between 6 a.m. and 5.30 pm and which even in 1907, and which was stated as 18. A further note in October 1936 commenting, " .....authority was given for the gang to be increased by 1 Lengthman as intervals between trains did not permit the use of car and trolley". Evidence then that the economic system could only satisfactorily be applied where there was both the likely of a saving over a realistic period, and also where the train service was not so intense.

Another Devon branch dealt with in 1907 was the Moretonhampstead line brought into use on 29th April. At this time two gangs of six men each replaced the previous four gangs of four men in each. Here also the gangs lengths did not correspond exactly with the electric train staff sections. Sometime prior to 1914 a modification was made to the lengths and the line covered by three gangs. (Presumably then an additional velocipede, mechanical trolley, watch and oilskins were provided, but this is not mentioned). Later still in December 1929 an increase in the complement of one gang by one man was authorised. The reason for this was stated to be responsibility for additional maintenance of sidings at Newton Abbot. One final change noted was the repositioning of the first key box out from Newton Abbot from its original site at 76 chains to a new position at 48 chains, this took place on 8th April 1926.

The Moretonhampstead line would retain basic economic maintenance throughout its existence although the adjoining Teign Valley branch from Heathfield through Exeter was only equipped with the Motor Economic system.

In neighbouring Cornwall, the short line from Lostwithiel to Carne Point Signal Box near Fowey was equipped and brought into use on 7th May 1907. The saving was just one man at £44 4s per year and on paper would take three years to recover. In addition though the new gang of four men also took on responsibility for an additional 69 chains as far as Carne Point whilst the neighbouring Gang No 160 additionally lost a post in consequence. The saving on cost consequent upon the reduction in strength to Gang 160 was not included in the figures. The route was worked by electric train staff (- standard Webb & Thompson manufacture), and equipped with eight telephones, five being in newly erected huts alongside the line.

What was officially known as the Severn Valley Line south of Shrewsbury came next, although only as far south as Highley. Even so this was a track distance of over 28 miles and when loops and sidings were included, involved responsibility for maintenance of over nearly 37 miles of track – see tables commencing on next page for the exact measurements. The obvious question at this stage must be why not continue the new arrangements south through to at least Bewdley? The answer to this is contained in a note within the Paddington Record, "It was suggested that Economic System should be applied between 137m 60ch Bewdley and 171m 55 ¾ch Burnt Mill Jc, but the Superintendent of the Line expressed a doubt whether the train service would admit of the system being worked with advantage at the Bewdley end: and it was decided to apply the arrangement between Highley and Burnt Mill Junction only". In making this decision both here and as regards the suitability of other lines due regard had to be paid not only to the frequency of the train service but also the length of the single line sections. Gangers' occupation never was permitted until the train had cleared the section and the 'token' returned to the instrument. As far as the Severn Valley line was concerned, the figures quoted state the previous manning level had been nine gangs totalling 41 men, but it was also noted that this level had already been reduced by three men in July 1905. (Presumably then the figure of 41 referred to the revised figure allowing for the reduction?) The new arrangements were split into six gangs and was commenced on 23rd September 1907. It is believed the original economic maintenance remained in use between Highley and Buildwas for the life of the railway. North of Buildwas the route through to Burnt Mill Junction was subsequently converted to Motor Operation.

The area around Monmouthshire was the final installation of 1907 covering the line from Ross through Monmouth as far as Little Mill Junction. At the same time as this installation was taking place, work was also proceeding on the adjoining Wye Valley branch from Monmouth as far south as Wye Valley Junction near Chepstow, although in the event this latter installation was not completed until early 1908. Even so it is convenient to group the descriptions of both lines together.

Dealing first with the longer route from Ross to Little Mill Junction, a precursor to the economic system was the installation of Webb-Thompson Electric Train Staff operation in place of the existing Train Staff and Ticket arrangement. This was at an estimated cost of £565 and, as elsewhere, is not otherwise included in the cost of the installation. Nine gangs were now replaced by just six, a saving of six men overall. Again, as elsewhere with large installations, the original gang lengths also did not correspond with the 'staff' sections. The new working commenced on 7th October 1907.

On the Wye Valley Branch a similar change to the Electric Train Staff was necessary first with the comment, "The alteration to Electric Train Staff working involved an increase in Traffic Dept expenses of £18 4s per annum owing to the necessity for employing an adult Signal Porter instead of a Lad Porter at Tidenham". At the time of installation, 6th January 1908, the previous manning of four gangs totalling 17 men was reduced to two gangs totalling 13 men. A further note describing a subsequent alteration noted, "Consequent upon the closing of Tidenham Station, Mr. Blackall states, (letter dated 30.3.1917) that the section of line between Wye Valley Junction and Tintern is now working in one group instead of two as previously". Assuming that two gangs still remained, from the above it would appear then that the gang lengths were altered to one of 4 miles 51 chains and a second of 8 miles 37 chains, no doubt a redistribution of manpower then also occurring.

It was now some seven months before another line was ready to commence working in the revised fashion and which may be taken to read that the first flush of suitable branches had already been dealt with. As will be related this was indeed the case, for the next installation on the Whitland and Cardigan branch between Boncarth and Cardigan was to be an impractical installation and was one of several where alterations had to be made as the original installation proved both impractical and unpopular.

Between Boncarth and Cardigan the new arrangements were brought into use on 31st August 1908 and involved the provision of ten telephone huts. The section was also now maintained by one gang instead of two, but the savings did not just relate to the loss of a single ganger, for a reduction in grade of one man from Leading Packer to Packer also occurred which meant the unfortunate individual was now paid 2/10d daily instead of his previous 3/-.

The earlier comment about the location of the telephones at the stations should be recalled at this stage for it is also clearly stated that, "an additional telephone has been provided in the Booking Office at Cardigan, in order that the Station Master may attend to the Ganger's calls at times when the Signal Porter is away from the Signal Cabin."

Why also only the final six and one-half miles of this branch should have been operated under the new arrangements is not reported, as there was also a further 18 and one-half miles also of single track. The gradient too on this longer section was similar, although there was a short section of 1 in 35 on the south side of Crymmych Arms.

(The Paddington Record gives 1 in 35 as the maximum gradient on the branch, although in so far as the section from Boncath to Cardigan was concerned and where the economic maintenance was installed, the maximum gradient was a slightly easier 1 in 40 albeit for some distance.)

The arrangements were superseded, it is believed, from 17th January 1927, at which time the following note appears, "In view of the difficulties experienced in working and the delays caused under the Economic System, it was decided to work the Branch under standard rules. By a re-arrangement of the gangs, it was found possible to reduce the manning on the Whitland & Cardigan Branch by two men". A slightly earlier note of November 1926, summarized matters more succinctly, "Owing to severe gradients combined with sharp curves, it was decided to abolish the Economic System on this branch".

This was the only time a comment appears in relation to delays to traffic being caused by the system and must then be taken to refer to possible difficulties in the use of the trolleys and distance between telephone points/ occupation key boxes. Perhaps this is slightly surprising as on the steepest gradient, that immediately leaving Boncath, the key boxes were located no more than 58 chains apart, and implying such consideration had been given at time the installation was planned.

Even so the GWR was not to be defeated, for later on 25th September 1933, the complete line from Cardigan Junction – bar the first few chains, all the way through to Cardigan itself was taken into the Motor Economic System. Whether the original key huts and telephones north of Boncath had been retained on site and were re-used is not reported, although it is known the velocipede car and trolley had by now been taken away.

The next route was also in Wales but this time further south and involved what was officially referred to as the 'Carmarthen and Cardigan Branch (Section Pencader to Newcastle Emlyn)". The Paddington Record gives justification and explanation for the installation which affords an interesting insight into the thinking of the time, "It was originally intended to work under the Economic System between Abergwili Junc and Newcastle Emlyn; but owing to complications arising from the switching out of Pencader Tunnel Signal Box during part of the day and at night, it was impractical to arrive at a satisfactory arrangement. In view of this and of the accelerated service of trains to Aberystwyth which passes over this Branch between Abergwili Junc and Pencader Junc it was decided to deal with the portion from Pencader Junc to Newcastle Emlyn only. See papers K.67809/48".

From this description the impression is given that the whole line to Newcastle Emlyn was part of an important through route. In point of fact this only applied to the line from Carmarthen to Aberystwyth, as a glance at any contemporary railway map of the area will reveal the Newcastle Emlyn section as a dead end branch.

The new arrangements afforded the opportunity to consolidate the previous three gangs involving 14 men into two gangs totalling 12 men. The posts of Ganger and Leading Packer were now redundant saving £54 12s and £46 16s respectively per annum.

The number of new installations was now diminishing fast, none being completed in 1909 and just two in 1910. Of these the first involved the Marlborough Branch in Wiltshire, a steeply graded line running just under five and one-half miles from a junction with the main west of England line (- at this point known as the Berks and Hants Extension Railway), to a terminus at the Wiltshire town. Marlborough was of course also served by the independent Midland & South Western Junction system but there would be no physical connection between the two at Marlborough for some years to come.

The Marlborough branch is shown as being fitted with five intermediate telephone huts each with an Occupation Key instrument, although only telephones are referred to as being provided at Savernake and Marlborough stations. The line was worked by Electric Train Staff.

Brought into use on 1st August 1910, there was an annual saving of £109 4s calculated on the basis of a single gang of six men compared with the earlier arrangement of two gangs of four. The branch continued to be maintained in the same way until closed in March 1933. Although no date is given in the Paddington Record, this was very likely to have been the date on which closure took place, the 6th March.

The second line completed in 1910 – although in the Paddington Record the entry precedes that of Marlborough, was the Launceston branch between Tavistock and Launceston. This is shown as having commenced operation from 26th December 1910, a slightly earlier date of 10th December 1909 being crossed through. This time, why just a section of line was dealt with is not reported and instead the entries give basic factual information and little else. We are told that five gangs of men were now maintaining the line compared with the previous six which equated to 20 men. This effected a saving of five posts and equivalent to £237 18s each year. Further economy was also achieved in manpower effective November 1926 when the five gangs were reduced still further to four and made up of two each of five and two of four men. In 1910 we also know that each ganger was provided with a separate Velocipede with which to inspect his section daily, presumably from 1926 these inspection lengths would have been increased which made one of the inspection vehicles and mechanical trolleys spare? At both time periods, 1910 and 1926, the gangers sections did not correspond with the Electric Train Staff sections.

The year 1911 witnessed just one installation, involving the complete length of the Bridport branch from its junction at Maiden Newton through Bridport and on to West Bay. At the time this line was reported as having a variety of types of rail, predominantly of flange type and more demanding then as regards maintenance. Despite this it was stated that the new arrangement would permit the previous three gangs to be replaced by two totalling 12 men and so saving two posts. Additionally one man was also to be dispensed with from the Weymouth line – due to part of the branch, 1m 21ch, previously being looked after by two of the main line gangs. The new arrangement meant the branch gangs would now cater for the whole line. It was noted that there was also one temporary man who would be retained until the flange rail was replaced.

The scheme was brought into use on 5th June 1911 and so it is believed continued unaltered until 28th January 1937 when the section between Bridport and West Bay reverted to 'Telephone' occupation. This was as a result of the withdrawal of electric train staff working between these locations. The remainder of the line continued as before until 17th May 1938 when it was noted, "Mr. Page reported no use was being made of the Key system". Accordingly is noted shortly afterwards that, "The mechanical trolley system on the branch was abandoned 22nd July 1938".

The last four routes to be discussed at this stage were all brought into operation in either 1912 or 1913, the confusion affecting the very last, the Lambourn branch, will be mentioned shortly. They are also not necessarily all in chronological sequence in the Paddington Record and so in date order should start with the Chard branch.

Here the equipment was installed to a point at 12 miles 61 chains which point marked the end of GWR maintenance, responsibility passing then to the LSWR. Originally marked as worked by 'Train Staff and Ticket', this was crossed out and replaced by 'Electric Train Staff', confirmation coming in an additional note that this change had been approved by the Traffic Committee for an estimated cost of £600.

The detailed description also refers to six telephones that were installed in stations and signal boxes. In the latter category there were only five signal boxes on the line, namely Creech Junction, Thornfalcon, Hatch, Ilminster, and Chard. A note stated that Hatch was switched out and only opened as required. Consequently it may well have been that the additional telephone was installed at Hatch station.

Perhaps the most interesting aspect of the installation was the cost. '12 huts with telephones and Occupation Key Instruments' and also the additional six telephones previously referred to. The cost of these was some £450, at an average of £25 per installation, the highest to date. It may be that this was the first time Control Instruments had been factored in to the cost from the outset, although to add even further confusion the new gang lengths corresponded reasonably with the 'staff' sections on the branch and although not having their boundaries exactly opposite the signal boxes could well have been within station limits and therefore under the protection of fixed signals.

The previous arrangement of four gangs was therefore replaced by three and with 15 men working instead of the previous 20. The Chard branch commenced its revised method of operating on 17th June 1912.

An estimated financial saving of £301 12s per annum and equivalent to six men was also achieved when a large part of the Barnstaple branch, between Dulverton and Barnstaple, was converted and brought into use on 30th September 1912.

Five gangs were now involved in maintaining the line compared to the previous six and although five velocipedes are referred to, the annotation distinctly states just four Mechanical Trolleys were supplied. For the first time also these latter items are reported as having, '...low gear and arrangements for disconnecting handle', which meant that advantage could be taken of a favourable gradient – the ruling gradient on the line being 1 in 58. It is not known if existing trolleys supplied to other lines in the past were, or even could be modified in like fashion. (There does not appear to be any written rule appertaining to the maximum speed of a mechanical trolley or other trolley, and which in the 1913 GWR Rule Book was in fact referred to as a 'lorry'. Certainly the Rule Book was very clear in later years that the speed of a Motor Trolley should not exceed 20mph, although it should be remembered that no speedometer was ever fitted to either the hand or motor versions).

Next came what was referred to as the 'Lampeter and Aberayron Light Railway'. It would appear this was originally scheduled to have 14 telephone huts and instruments and three additional telephones in 'stations and signal boxes'. Even before the system had been brought into use, though a modification was made to just six lineside installations and so the cost was quoted at £262 10s compared with the £360 10s originally envisaged. The proposed reduction in manning of two men to 12 although retaining the two gangs on the branch was not altered. The system was brought into use on 11th November 1912. A further change to this line was reported in October 1926 when the provision of one further key box at 6 miles 55 chains near Felin Fach (previously known as Ystrad), permitted a further reduction of one Underman in the strength of the gang responsible for the section from that point through to Aberayron.

We come now to the final line to be considered at this stage, the Lambourn branch running for just under 12 miles through the valley of the same name to its terminus. Confusion relative to this installation has already been hinted at, and which starts right from the outset with dispute over the installation date, 1st September 1913 written in pen and in the usual hand and which also corresponds with the same style for the remainder of the entry. Annotated above though but in pencil is a different date, 23rd September 1912. The new arrangement of two gangs each of five men also corresponded exactly with the Electric Tablet sections operating on the branch and meaning the gangs met at the mid way point, viz Welford Park. A saving of two men was achieved under the new arrangement.

For whatever reason though, it appears that as time passed the equipment was little used, which was explained by a note of October 1928, "Owing to the limited use made of the Economic System, the scheme was abandoned on the Branch on....(no day given) October 1928, when the former manning of 3 Gangs of 4 men each was resorted to on the 3rd December 1928".

As recounted previously, this was not of course the

only line to revert to conventional operating although clearly this could only have been achieved with some form of official sanction, the preferences of the men themselves hardly likely to have had much effect.

Up to the start of 1914, 39 lines or sections of lines had been dealt with and it would appear an overall appraisal was taken by Paddington of a number of the remaining branches where consideration might be given to further expansion of the system. No division of the GWR was excluded and from the accompanying comments it is also perhaps easier to see which of the Divisional Engineers were in favour and which perhaps not so keen.

The appraisal entries were spread over two sides and form a separate set of loose pages within the Paddington Record, headed "Light Branch Lines where Economic System has not been brought into operation". For the sake of ease of reading the statistical analysis for the lines, within each engineering Division they are grouped together. Additionally a few later comments on similar subjects were made at odd points within the Paddington Register around 1926, when it appears a handful of lines were again brought up for discussion. For the sake of completeness these are included under the relevant divisional in this section and annotated accordingly.

Wiveliscombe, on the Barnstaple branch from Taunton. An early form of motorised inspection trolley is seen making its way through the platform with, in the distance, the signalman poised ready to receive the return of the occupation key. (Although it could equally be the token for the single line, if the ganger had run all the way between token stations.) The date is as late as 29 April 1961, yet in reality little would have changed for some decades - although all would be swept with the wholesale closure of so many lines in the next few years. The photograph is included to illustrate several points, firstly the type of line used for the economic (and later the motor-economic) system of maintenance: branch and single line cross country routes. Next the progression from a pump-action inspection vehicle to what was a petrol-engined machine - note the headlight, and finally how the effects of war with the alternate white-edge to the platform was still being repainted years later. Much of the Barnstaple branch was upgraded to the 'motor' system in 1933 - see page 55.
Mark Warburton, courtesy Mrs Margaret Warburton.

In 1914 an assessment was made of branch and secondary lines (by division) on which the system had not been installed. Divisional engineers were also asked their reasons for not including these routes.

The Divisional Reports (Divisional Engineer's comments - where made - appended underneath.

Division	**Branch**	**Length (Total mileage including sidings)**	**How Worked**	**No of Trains between 6. am and 5.30 pm (occasional in brackets)**	**Maximum gradient**	**Minimum curve (Radius in chains)**	**No of Gangs**	**No of Men**
London	Marlow	2m 60ch (3m 69ch)	Electric Train Staff	28 (4)	132	7	1	5
	Didcot to Newbury	17m 15ch (19m 19ch)	Electric Train Staff	13 (5)	106	14	6	24
	Newbury to Winchester	25m 74 ch (31m 29.5ch)	Electric Train Staff	13 (2)	106		9	37
	Wallingford	2m 37.25ch "m 79.75ch)	Train Staff	24	202	11	1	3
	Abingdon	2m 50ch (3m 67.5ch)	Train Staff	28 (2)	200	10	1	4
	Faringdon (part of branch included in another gang)	3m 37ch (4m 14ch)	Train Staff assisted by Block Telegraph	20	86	15	1	4

Didcot – Newbury / Newbury Winchester – Mr. J.N. Taylor wrote on 9/2/1905, 'Certainly could not recommend new system be adopted on Didcot & Winchester Line. We have all our work cut out to keep lines in good order now that fast trains are running over them and a considerable portion of the road is of flange rails secured by clips to sleepers'.

Wallingford – General Manager informed on 16/3/1904 that recent reductions had been made below which it would hardly be possible to go (?) if Electric Staff working and occupation keys were introduced.

Division	Branch	Length	How Worked	No of Trains	Maximum gradient	Minimum curve	No of Gangs	No of Men
Bristol	Calne	5m 21ch (6m 21ch)	Electric Train Staff	17	60	9	2	9
	Cheddar Valley	17m 35ch (24m 9.25ch)	Electric Train Staff	17 (2)	75	14	6	25
	Wells to Witham	13m 22ch (15m 39.25ch)	Electric Train Staff	16 (2)	46	14	4	17
	Portishead		Electric Train Staff	21 (3)	100	12	3	21
	Clevedon		Electric Train Staff	27	249	7	1	5
	Camerton – Limpley Stoke		Electric Train Tablet	10 (1)	50	11	3	15
	Avonmouth		Train Staff & Ticket / Electric Train Staff	3 (1)	160	15	3	14

Calne – Mr. W.K. Lawrence wrote on 11/4/1905, ' If telephone system is introduced I think an experiment might be made by reducing the strength by 1 man giving percentage 1.06 but this reduction should not be brought about until Vignole road has been removed. If branch is maintained by 1 Gang, the Ganger would be away from his men to extent it would seriously affect the strength of Gang'.

Wells to Witham – Mr. W.K. Lawrence stated on 27/11/1912 and 22/7/1913, 'New system impossible owing to heavy gradients, sharp curves. Could not properly be maintained with less men. It would also mean breaking up homes of 7 men and house accommodation is very scarce in this part of Somerset. Difficulty would be experienced regarding fogging arrangements'. (This and the next entry are the only times in the whole of the archive that the welfare of the staff is referred to).

Some years later in October 1926 the subject of introducing the system on this line was raised again. Again due to the gradients and also it was stated, the interval between trains, the matter was once more not proceeded with.

Camerton to Limpley Stoke – Mr. W.K. Lawrence stated on 27/11/1912 and 22/7/1913, 'New system impossible owing to heavy gradients, sharp curves. Could be not properly be maintained with less men. It would also mean breaking up homes of 4 men and house accommodation is very scarce in this part of Somerset. Difficulty would be experienced regarding fogging arrangements'.

in an even more rapid expansion of achieving economy through reduced cost. Such change could even be said to be an example of the type of economy both the railway industry and even society generally would experience in the latter decades of the twentieth century, and whilst not intending to imply a direct comparison, here were examples of technology replacing manpower so many years before.

The final stages of what was then still the hand operated economic maintenance began on 1st October 1918, and involved the Minsterley Branch from Cruckmeole Junction near Shrewsbury. The Paddington Record is also very scant in its recording of this new installation with only certain pencil notes compared to the detailed information once previously provided. Factual details are given in the table below and which also provides similar detail of the other conversions up to 1933.

The final installations of Economic Maintenance

Route / Branch	Route Length (maintained length in brackets)	Introduction of system	Type of rail originally provided	Number of telephones	Minimum radius curve (chains)	Maximum Gradient 1 in	Cost Estimate (actual)	Estimated Original Saving per annum	Note
Minsterley	4m 47ch (6.025ch)	1-1-1918?	Not Stated	2	Not Stated	100	£71	Not Stated	
Newent Branch	18m 30.5ch (19m 31.25ch)	15-8-1921	Bullhead	21	9	64	£2622	£920	Converted to Motor 27-10-1930.
Falmouth	11m 24ch	27-7-1921	Not Stated	17?	Not Stated	Not stated	£874 12s 6d	Not Stated	Partly converted to Motor 26-9-1932.
Dinas Mawddwy	6m 63ch (7m 22ch)	May 1926	Not stated	Not stated	Not stated	41	£19 10s	£19 4s	
Limpley Stoke to Hallatrow	Not stated	23-5-1927	Not stated	Not stated	100	10	£295	£668 4s	
Cirencester to Marlborough	26m 13ch (33m 68ch)	13-6-1927 and 20/6/1927	Not stated	30 (unconfirmed)	6	75	£3,365	£1,308	
Hallen Marsh - Pilning	5m 24ch (7m 45.5ch)	10-10-1927	Not stated	7	20	200	£580 (£467 10s 6d)	£517	
Whitchurch & Whittington	16m 67.75ch (21m 42.75ch)	28-11-1927	Not stated	18 (unconfirmed)	Not stated	80	£1,240	£530	Converted to Motor 21-1-1930
Andoversford Junction – Cirencester	13m 51.5ch	9-7-1928	Not stated	16	Not stated	Not stated	£1,080	£1,160	Converted to Motor 2-12-1929
Clynderwen - Letterston									Note 1
Dolgelley – Barmouth Junction	7m 31ch	15-4-1929	Not stated	8	Not stated	Not stated	£550 (£409 11s 9d)	£260	Converted to Motor 9-4-1934
Cleobury Mortimer – Ditton Priors	12m 5ch (13m 75.75ch)	27-3-1933	Not stated	13	Not stated	Not stated	£285	£200 18s	

1. The reference to an economic installation on this line is not to be found in the Paddington Record and instead was noted in a GWR Engineering Department register at the time lodged at Porchester Road. It was stated approval was given on 25th October 1928 for an estimated cost of £390 but then a further entry refers to additional telephones for £550. Credence is given to the likelihood the system was installed at an actual cost of £883 17s.

As far as the Minsterley branch was concerned, the only cost quoted was for two telephones, four occupation key instruments and two boxes to house the telephones. This came to £71. It was also stated that a spare mechanical trolley was utilised but that a velocipede was not provided – but again see later! A further interesting note commented, "Under standard rules, this branch was maintained by one gang of six men. One man however was (and is) occupied almost entirely in pumping for the Locomotive Department at Minsterley and it is anticipated that the Economic System actually introduced on account of shortage of staff during the War, will obviate the necessity for an additional man", - hence the date of introduction is uncertain. But, a surviving copy of the notice advising staff of the introduction of the working does tend to contradict matters somewhat in that it states a velocipede is provided. This handbill though would appear to have been in effect a standard note for all installations of the Economic System of Maintenance from about 1907 onwards. The mention of the Minsterley Branch being a joint line is of further interest in that this is believed to have been the only joint line on which the system was installed.

At this stage too it may perhaps be appropriate to digress slightly relative to the general manpower situation as applied to the GWR after 1918. From official statistics there were some 76,480 GWR staff in 1913. Of these 22,955 volunteers for war service at some stage between 1914 and 1918 – indeed despite railwaymen being in a reserved occupation, it was *expected* that men would volunteer. (A relevant tangent is that it was only if a man had volunteered and been rejected, or had served and then been discharged, that he would be issued with a GWR Railway Service badge.)

This proportion of GWR men serving with the forces amounted then to a little over 30% of the total available work force and whilst many of these were of course replaced by women for the duration, every department suffered both staff shortages and difficulties due to lack of experience.

This would similarly take time to redress with a return to peace and it may well have been then that staff shortage allied to inflation meant that certain routes were now considered as viable for the economic system compared with previously. The inflation aspect was also no doubt a feature of consideration relative to subsequent conversions in later years as well.

Finally it should be mentioned that out of those 22,955, 20,431 men returned to GWR service (2,524 died, representing a 12% loss of those who joined the forces), although a further unknown number were no longer in the best of rude health and consequently unable to partake in their previous role. Here the GWR was a considering employers and a number of men found lesser employment on the railway although naturally at a lesser wage. But it was better than nothing.

A further breakdown of these figures relative to the Engineering Department is not possible, neither is a similar analysis for the lines covered by this work. Finally at this stage it should be mentioned that other railway companies suffered similar losses, although it is generally accepted that in proportionate terms more GWR men volunteered as a proportion to the total staffing levels than on any other UK railway.

Back to the main subject of this work, and the next line dealt with was the Falmouth Branch from 27th July 1921. Detail on this installation is also unusual in that the only record of this comes from a handbill and memo within the Paddington Record but with no other information save a page number which is then blank!

Falmouth was strange in several respects, firstly because the initial few chains on the branch from Penwithers Junctions were double track, but mainly because the introduction notice clearly states that there were either three or four keys per group. The full explanation of this is not certain but it may be assumed that one or more keys could be removed per section simultaneously although the section could not be restored until all keys had been returned. Taking the first Group, Penwithers Junction to Perranwell as an example, there were presumably key boxes in the signal boxes at either end as well. This then makes a total of six available key boxes for which there were three keys. The Ganger thus had to ensure that the key was returned to an empty box, or was this where the illusive lozenge shaped occupation key instrument box was installed that could accommodate two keys? (The Falmouth installation was originally estimated at £108 for the Engineering Department and £825 to the 'Telegraph' (?) department – did they really mean Signal Department? The actual figure though was a total between the departments of £874 12s 6d.)

It is believed this method of working with multiple keys gave by far the most flexible occupation under the key system and was installed in connection with the pending replacement of the numerous wooden viaducts on the Falmouth line. Whether a similar system was installed around the same time on other lines in the area where maintenance was high due to the pre-existing timber viaducts, is not known. Similarly was the multi-key system retained throughout the life of the branch installation? All that is known is that the section from Perranwell to Falmouth was subsequently converted to motor operation just over a decade later. (As will be gathered, date wise the Paddington Register is by now nowhere near as accurate in its recording of detail as it had been previously. Another 'hand' is also clearly tasked with maintaining the records although possibly they were by now also kept elsewhere. Some of the information then after this time has had to be gleaned from alternative primary sources and whilst corroboration has been attempted whenever possible, it is not quite the same as knowing all the information was in place and just from a single source.)

In addition to a handbill and notice, a further instruction was issued locally by the Divisional Superintendent relative to the Falmouth line on 8th November 1921:

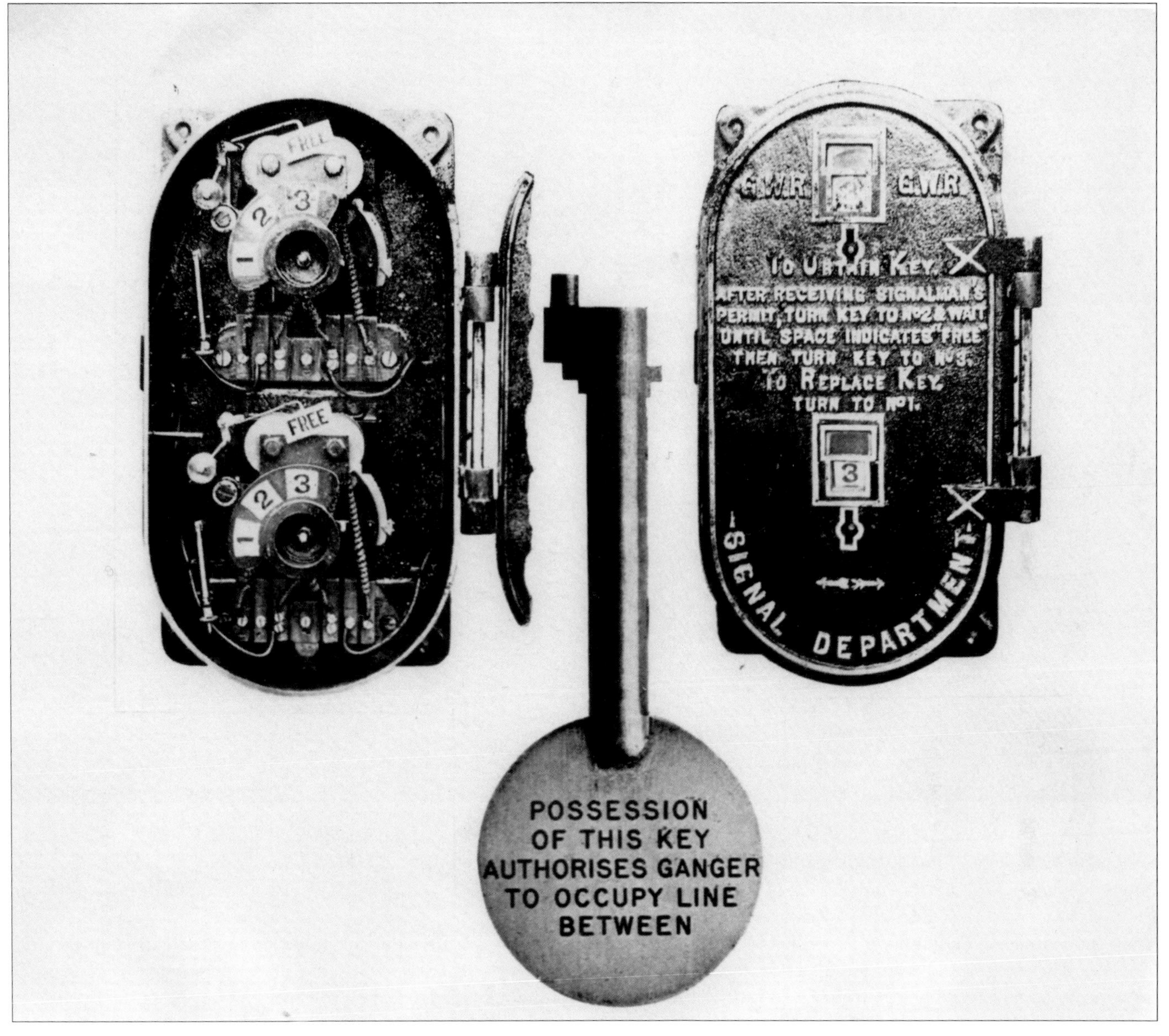

An illustration which has (and remains) an enigma. It is included in the hope that someone may be able to assist in its identification. Clearly a GWR Occupation Key instrument but one where two keys - note of the same configuration - might be used. The author has never seen one of these instruments 'in the flesh' and its use must be open to question. At first glance it might have been thought to be the type of machine where two separate gangs would meet, each having to insert their respective key before the line could be restored, except that under these circumstances the gangs would be certain to have keys of a differing configuration. The image dates from the early years of the 20th century and as such precedes by many years the one section of double line on the GWR, Crudgington - Peplow, that was maintained under 'occupation key' and then only in the days of the later 'Motor Economic System'. At the present time the only consistent solution might be that this was for an early experiment where two keys were provided for the same occupation key section with both having to be restored into machines before normal train working might be restored. The gang involved would then be able to work in two separate locations simultaneously. If this were the case it was a feature that was later considered unnecessary for the members of a gang could all work perfectly safely in any number of locations provided the single key was not restored until all work had been completed. The shape of the instrument will also be noted.

"When an Occupation Key will be required during the time the Branch is closed, the flagman at the site of work will proceed to the nearest Occupation Key Hut immediately after the passing of the last train on the preceding evening, for the purpose of withdrawing such key, and will lock same up in the box provided for the purpose in the hut. Keys of this Box will be held by the Flagman and the Ganger, and the latter will obtain the occupation key before commencing work in the morning. The occupation key must be restored to the instrument at least 15 minutes before the first booked

Pump truck, out of use and stored at Stratton on the erstwhile Highworth branch. Photographed well into BR days, this shows that equipment such as this was often still to be found, very occasionally still in use, but certainly to be seen derelict and abandoned long after it had ceased to be in regular service. *Austin Attewell*

train is due to leave Falmouth or Penwithers Jcn".

The next installation involved a section of line previously considered, namely from Over Junction towards Ledbury and referred to as the 'Newent Branch'. This time it was not just part of the line as far Dymock that was considered but instead the whole branch from Over Junction through to Ledbury was dealt with. The system was introduced on Monday 15th August 1921. The costs quoted in the accompanying table, £2,622 also give some idea of how inflation had taken effect over the ensuing years whilst for the first time also a figure for contingencies is also allowed for, in this case £38 3s and possibly inserted to take into account the potential for further inflationary rises occurring between the time of the estimate at authorisation and the actual figure later applied. (No other costings are given). The total figure was also spilt between the Signal Department – who provided the Occupation Key instruments and telephones, and the Engineering Department, for the actual permanent way equipment. The anticipated saving of £920 was achieved through reducing the previous six gangs to four.

Control instruments would also certainly have been provided from the outset as per the comment, "The staff sections are divided into three groups, and the Gangers of Groups 98 and 99 are able to obtain occupation simultaneously on the Newent – Over Junction Section". Incidentally this appears to be referred to contemporaneously as "Special Occupation". "Ordinary Occupation" being in force elsewhere on the route. This was also the final installation before the "Grouping of Railways", after which it would be almost five years before another line was dealt with.

This gap in years is probably explained by a practical limit on the number of lines that could be realistically operated in the manner described – as per the 1914 assessment. But, as touched on previously, changing traffic and operational patterns allied to increased costings may well have been the trigger to reassess previously unconsidered routes.

Such was probably the case of the branch from Cemmes Road to Dinas Mawddwy and which was also the first installation on a line now under Great Western control consequent upon the Grouping.

The branch to Dinas Mawddwy was worked on the 'one engine in steam' principle using a Train Staff, and it was stated involving a maximum of seven trains – all of which ran 'mixed' during the usual daylight hours. The Paddington Record again includes the usual coloured drawing, although as mentioned, both it and the accompanying text are nowhere near as ornate as in the earliest years, and also prepared by a different hand – but this was of course now over 20 years since the records in the book had been commenced.

Interestingly the installation was referred to as a 'Modified form of the Economic System', and which was explained thus; "No occupation key instruments installed, and, there is no Signal Dept work involved as telephones already exist at Cemmes Road, and Dinas Mawddwy Stations, and at a Grocer's Shop close to Aberangell Station. The telephone service is understood to be used exclusively for Company's service, all this maintained by the Post Office".

With equipment then only provided by the Engineering Department, the cost was also bound to be considerably reduced, and so equated to just £19.10s – the Velocipede amounting to £17 15s alone. It was further stated that a spare Mechanical Trolley was available for use so this was not included in the cost.

The revised arrangement was estimated to save the wages of two temporary men who were employed for four weeks per annum, and meaning maintenance would now be carried out by a single gang of five men at a wages cost of £642 4s annually.

The branch would be destined to be maintained by the new arrangements for only just over eight years as on 3rd December 1934 the following note appeared, "Thus branch now comes under the supervision of Motor Gang No 48 Llanbrynmair – the mechanical Trolleys have been withdrawn (- in this respect referring to the velocipede and gangers trolley) as the gang may use the motor vehicles over the Branch provided the Ganger has the Train Staff in his possession". This latter situation on this branch is also referred to again briefly in Chapter 7.

Another line where a modified form of Economic Maintenance was introduced, was that referred to as the 'Limpley Stoke to Hallatrow Branch' and which came into the scheme from 23rd May 1927. (Known also as the Camerton Branch.)

As with other lines previously described in the Paddington Register, the wealth of discussion appertaining to this installation affords a wonderful look back at the rationale appertaining to the line and which commenced, "There is now no passenger train service and the one Goods Train per day in each direction, on the above branch, and a modified form of economic system of maintenance has been introduced whereby the Engineering Department have daily occupation of the line from 4.0 pm to 10.0 am the following day".

Details were then given as to the previous manning arrangements – three gangs totalling 15 men, and which would be reduced under the new system to two gangs of four, producing an annual wage saving of £668 4s. Costs were sub-divided as being £160 to the Signal Department relative to the provision of Occupation Key Boxes at Camerton and Hallatrow Signal Boxes and, "...necessary alterations to telephonic system to enable remainder of branch to be worked by telephones". The remainder of the estimated cost, £135, was against the Engineering Department for "Velocipedes, Trolleys, Huts etc".

However, even before the limited work prescribed above was carried out, a further note appeared, "It was later found that the Occupation Key Boxes, were not required at Hallatrow and Camerton, and there was no Signal Department work to do. All that was necessary was to supply the Gangers with Keys to enable them to gain admittance to the existing telephones at the various places.

The plan within the Paddington Record is also contradictory in giving details of the "staff sections", Hallatrow – Camerton, Camerton – Dunkerton, and Dunkerton – Limpley Stoke, but is this in some respect contradicted by a note which speaks of "tablet" from Camerton to Hallatrow, and "Wooden Staff" – Limpley Stoke and Camerton. Four key boxes are also indicated but in view of the above it is unlikely these were installed.

The limited use made of the line indicated still further economy in working, and which in July 1928 saw the gangs reduced to three men in each. This was reduced still further to a single gang of five men in October 1928 then based at Hallatrow. A final reduction occurred in June 1931 with the combining of three men from the Hallatrow gang with another gang. It was intended that one man, acting as sub-ganger, would then examine the Camerton to Limpley Stoke section three times weekly on a velocipede car, although it is not certain this last amendment took place as the final entry, in pencil, and dated 18th September 1931, simply stated, "not yet effected".

The basic type of telephone occupation referred to on this line was not of course unlike that seen very early on, and indeed worked well provided all involved complied with the regulations, tragedy possibly occurring when they did not – Shipston branch. A fortunately less serious incident occurred on an unreported date between Monkton Combe and Limpley Stoke, and which is described in *The Camerton Branch*, "Branch trains were not allowed to leave Limpley Stoke until the ganger had arrived back on the velocipede. When he reached Monkton Combe on his way back from Camerton, he telephoned Limpley Stoke to inform the signalman that he was on his way. This action allowed the train to proceed from Limpley Stoke South signal box to the North signal box, to await his arrival. On one occasion, the porter/signalman at the north box assumed that the ganger had arrived and allowed the train to proceed onto the branch. Beyond Fisher's Crossing, the velocipede speeding down the hill, crashed into the train, the ganger jumping clear. The remains of the velocipede were then placed in the brake van!"

Another piece of folklore from the same source describes an incident which was surely not confined to this line, "At one period a velocipede was kept at Camerton and a porter, knowing the whereabouts of the key which locked it, used this vehicle as a most unusual conveyance to a dance at Combe Hay. It was locked to the rails while the hop was on and then used for his return journey!"

Largest of all the post first world war economic installations was that affecting part of the former MSWJ line between Cirencester to Marlborough and which was brought into use in two stages. Firstly that between Cirencester to Swindon – just under 15 miles, instigated on 13th June 1927, and with the second section between Swindon and a point just north of Marlborough dealt with so as to commence the new working on 20th June 1927.

It should also be mentioned at this stage that this installation on the former MSWJ was also the first to be converted to the new 'Motor Economic System of Maintenance' less than a year later.

Due to the total length of line involved and in consequence the detail that was required on the drawing showing the proposed position of the telephone huts, revised gang lengths, and 'staff sections', a pull out drawing was provided in the Paddington Register although in other respects the information was as before – even if there was more of it!

Possibly even at the time the original installation was being proposed, thoughts were indeed looking towards the revised 'motor' scheme which would follow, as a note states, "The average distance between telephones was extended from 58 chains to about 70 chains, thus affecting a saving in seven boxes and instruments. This with the substitution of telephone boxes for telephone huts affected a saving on the original vote of over £490". – this is also the first mention of a 'telephone hut', and may well be the type of installation later seen in the earlier illustrations.

As such the original estimate of £2,665 for instruments and telephones was reduced accordingly, whilst in February 1928 it was reported that the Signal Engineer had advised that a saving of £1,431 had been effected through "...simplifying the system and utilising 2nd hand telephones", - possibly the simplification was that referred to in increasing the telephone distances. A further £700 was attributable to the Engineering Department for the, "Velocipede Cars, Mechanical Trolleys, Huts etc" – although similarly reduced without explanation to £419. This meant the original estimate of £3,365 eventually came out at an actual figure of £1,653.

The revised manpower figures showed that the original nine gangs were now reduced to six, with a net saving of 11 men, or £1,308 in wages annually.

Another interesting first comment noted, "By installing a 'loud speaker' in each of the Signal Boxes, controlling the Occupation Key System, the Ganger, or other person in charge of the occupation key can communicate with the signalman without surrendering the occupation of the line, or restoring the occupation key in the instrument". Does this then mean that on previous installations the reverse was the case? By inference perhaps yes, although if so it would certainly have appeared to have been a somewhat convoluted arrangement.

No details were given as to the number of velocipedes or inspection cars provided, although it was stated that Gang No 133 Swindon – Ganger and four men, is not provided with either vehicle as they only maintain a short section – 2miles 6.25chains, north of Swindon Town. This was also one of the few occasions that the actual Engineering Gang numbers were quoted on the plan that accompanied the Paddington Record.

The sections, Ogbourne to Chiseldon, Swindon 'A' to Rushey Platt, and Rushey Platt to Cricklade, were also noted as those where two keys were provided, and which was explained as , "...to enable the Gangers of adjoining gangs within a staff section to obtain occupation at the same time". Aside from on the Falmouth branch, referred to previously, this was the only other confirmed installation up to this time where more than one key was provided, although it is likely the two keys were a different configuration. Others though would follow, seemingly also ever more involved as Reading developed more sophisticated installations.

Part of the Avonmouth Branch, that between Hallen Marsh to Pilning Junction came next, with the new working introduced from 10th October 1927. This short branch had previously occupied two gangs of five men at a wage cost of £1,284 per annum. The new arrangement seeing a single gang of six men and an annual saving of £517.

The estimated cost of installation was only £580 and so would be recouped in just over a single year. This installation cost was made up of £470 to the Signal Department, "Providing occupation key system to be available when either the Electric Train Staff or Token is in use and telephones worked on the same principle as those introduced on the MSW Jcn Section". With only one gang though this could still mean two keys so allowing members of the gang to work safely at two separate locations on the line.

Engineering Department work accounted for the £110 – velocipede, trolley and huts, although this was reduced by utilising the two wheeled vehicles redundant from the abandonment of the system on Whitland to Cardigan Branch earlier in 1927.

Shortly after Avonmouth came the line between Whitchurch and Whittington in Shropshire and which was brought into the new working arrangement from 28th November 1927. Converted to Motor 21st January 1930.

It is believed that a total of 18 key boxes was provided although the plan in the Paddington Record is not completely clear and suggesting instead that an additional two may have been installed. A key box was also originally shown at Oswestry, but this was not actually installed, the explanatory note simply stating, "Economic System will be terminated at Whittington".

Of the cost quoted, £1,030 was attributed to the Signal Department and the balance of £210 for 'Trolleys and huts'. The saving under the new working meant that three gangs totalling 18 men would now be involved compared with the previous four totalling 22 individuals. (In the light of the comment on savings made by using redundant trolleys on the Cirencester to Andoversford Junction section described next, it would appear that the

£210 mentioned may have meant that similar second hand vehicles were originally used here as well).

A second section of the former MSWJ line came next and this time north from Cirencester to Andoversford Junction. This occurred from 9th July 1928 and coincided also with the singling of this route from its previous double track status.

The actual number of key boxes and telephones provided was 16 and which would have made up the bulk of the £850 installation cost from the Signal Department. Just £230 being charged to the Engineering Department, and despite the three gangs each requiring one of each vehicle. It noted that, "It was found possible to effect a saving on the latter figure (- trolleys etc) by utilising redundant trolleys and cars for the use of the gangs", - this time it was not stated where they had originally emanated from.

The cost saving of £1,160 by reducing manning levels to 15 men in three gangs compared with the five gangs and 24 men should also be read carefully as the previous double line route here would naturally have required more maintaining. It is thought then that the savings referred to were calculated on the original maintenance cost.

The plan of the installation also gives details that the gang lengths did not correspond with the single line sections – worked it was said by electric tablet, and that consequently simultaneous possession was possible by neighbouring gangs either side of the signal boxes at Withington and Foss Cross. Three slide control instruments would have been installed in each of signal boxes mentioned.

Utilising basic economic maintenance north of Cirencester at this time is perhaps a little surprising as already south of Cirencester the newer 'Motor' system was in use. But as referred to previously, the line south of Cirencester was the first to be equipped with the revised working and so it was likely the Engineers wished to confirm the viability of the new arrangements before extending piecemeal.

The penultimate installation was that officially referred to as on the Dolgelley Branch between Dolgelley and Barmouth Junction and part of the former Cambrian Railways route, brought into use from 15th April 1929 – it is believed the work had been planned to be completed in January 1929.

This was also an extension of the earlier economic scheme on the line from Bala Junction brought into use by the GWR in December 1906 and which was described earlier. The new installation also saw changes to the manning in the gangs of the neighbouring earlier installation and consequently the annual saving quoted, £260, does not necessarily refer directly just to the line between Dolgelley and Barmouth Junction. Of the £550 installation cost, £450 was attributed to the Signal Department. The balance of £100 to the Engineering Department was probably costed mainly to the trolleys provided and likely to have been one of each.

The final line involved in the Economic System of Maintenance was that between Cleobury Mortimer and Ditton Priors and instigated on Monday 27th March 1933. This was also another basic installation with no key boxes and only telephones provided – as per Camerton and Shipston, the cost to the Signal Department then being just £90 for what is believed to have been 13 telephones. Justification for the work was given as the saving of two posts, and meaning ten men would now be employed instead of 12, although a note stated that, "Mr. Davis wrote on 24th November 1932 to the effect that only ten men had been employed on this branch for some months"). Even so there would now be two gangs instead of three.

The Engineering Department contribution was £195, and for two mechanical trolleys and two of what were then described as "velocipede cars", but it was also noted that, "It was possible to reduce this considerably by utilizing cars and trolleys recovered from the Much Wenlock branch", - partly converted to Motor trolley in 1931.

Preservation in both senses of the word. The signal box may now be enjoying a renewed lease of life but it is unlikely track maintenance on the Severn Valley will similarly revert.

Whether then this £195 was the original or revised figure is not clear.

This variation of economic maintenance on the Cleobury Mortimer and Ditton Priors line was destined to be short lived as the section was of course taken over by the Admiralty in September 1938 after which it was noted the system was, "in abeyance".

(Abridged from an unpublished manuscript of 80,000+ words covering the Economic and Motor Economic systems of maintenance by the present author.)

A Miscellany of Miscellanea

Late in the day on 15 May 1956 an electrical short-circuit caused a serious fire at Keysham & Somerdale East signal box. The signalman was injured and taken to hospital whilst the 'R.O.' reports two trains were delayed by a maximum of 75 minutes. The structure was condemned the following day. What signalling arrangements were in place for the next few weeks are not certain. A replacement 'non-standard' timber structure was commissioned and brought into use exactly two months after the fire on 15 July 1956. From the photographs and on the next page, it would appear the fire started below the operating floor and rapidly spread upwards. The smoke damage is apparent, especially to the walls and diagram. Still intact on the block shelf is a good representation of GWR equipment including 'single-deck' Spagnoletti instruments.

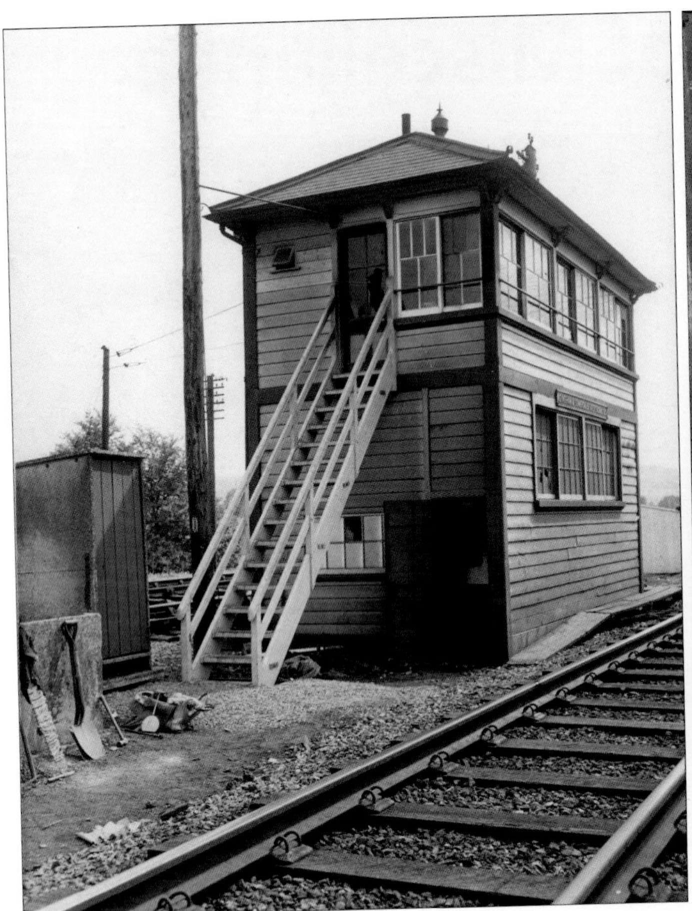

***Above, left -** From the opposite end at Keysham & Somerdale East , a cursory glance may give the impression all is well - until that is one observes the smoke-blackened windows and broken glass at this end of the operating floor. **Above right -** The photographer has recorded signal wires and pulleys, some of the former seemingly having come away from their mountings. Was this view taken to prove the seat of the blaze? If so, the only clue might be the inspection light with its burnt cable although this could well have been as a result of the inferno.*

...and speaking of signalling, one of several railway jobs that seem to have been rarely photographed was that of the signal maintenance engineer. Is this man simply posed for the camera or involved in the installation of or even the first steps of the removal of a signal arm? Regretfully no date or location to assist.

Above *- The practice of hiring a private saloon for a party - or even perhaps individual travel (?), was still extant well into BR days. Originally fitted out solely for ordinary First-Class travel, a number of saloons of the type seen were subsequently altered to cater for the transport of invalids. The illustration, obviously taken at Paddington, shows one of these. Originally built to Diagram G33 as a 'First-Class Bogie Saloon', from 1925, those vehicles converted to be able to cater for an invalid lying down, took on a revised diagram, D45. Ten vehicles had originally been built, four in 1900, two in 1903, and two separate batches of two in 1904. All were 47ft 6¾in long by 8ft 6¾ins wide. Some were also fitted with joint vacuum/Westinghouse brakes to be able to work off GW lines.*

Right *- 'Bob' the collecting dog from Stratford-on-Avon.*

Above *- Train guard switching off carriage lighting in compliance with black-out/air-raid warning.*

Left *- No 6947 , built as a 57ft 'Bars 2' single ended slip coach but subsequently rebuilt as a brake-composite: note the end windows are retained but the vehicle has had a gangway added as befits its new role. The churns/kegs being loaded are not identified.*

Right - *An unidentified 'Castle' on the final approaches to Paddington with train No '720', better known as 'The Red Dragon'.*

Bottom - *Modernisation comes to Gloucester. A publicity image from the 'Mercury Truck & Tractor Co. Ltd' (a Gloucester business), showing one of their tug units at work. Notice in the background the four banner-repeater signals informing of the indication of the signals for the crossovers midway along the platform.*

Opposite and above - *Topiary alongside the main line west of Paddington. Perhaps associated more with stations on quiet branch lines, the unusual nature of the location resulted in these 1935 images being submitted for possible inclusion in the 'Great Western Magazine' of the time.*

Right *- Divisional Engineers inspection train paused outside Whiteball tunnel signal box. A note accompanying the image quotes a date of 'Circa 1860' but this cannot be the case as the saloon seen (four were built) is likely to date from the early 1890s. The board on the front of the signal box reads, 'CATCH POINTS ARE SITUATED 40 YARDS OUTSIDE EAST END OF WHITEBALL TUNNEL.'* *See also p106.*

This page and opposite top *- Images of derailed vehicles are usually recording an unwanted incident. Here, though, a 20T coal wagon has been deliberately derailed on a sand-drag near Neath. The date and consequential assessment were not*

of the Country's economy. The Great Western Railway provided a vital transport link not only for passengers but also for mail, milk and other perishable goods between London, Midlands and the West of England. These services could not simply be suspended until the line had been cleared and the necessary forensic examinations completed; traffic was re-routed through Slough on the two relief lines while the down main line was cleared of wreckage and repaired. Remarkably this was completed and the line reopened to normal traffic before midnight the same day!

'The Official Investigation.'

Both the public and the GWR management were numb with shock by this seemingly inexcusable disaster. There had been no thick fog or blinding blizzard; instead of a rain lashed night it had been a glorious June afternoon. Even worse was the fact that the accident had happened on a straight and level railway belonging to a Company which had diligently built up such a reputation that it had become a watch word for passenger safety. Indeed, as one GWR official pointed out it had been ten years since a passenger had been killed on one of its trains.

The signalling at Slough incorporated some of the most modern equipment currently available. Slough East Signal Box's down main distant signal was electrically interlocked with the Slough Middle Signal Box's down main home signal and could only be lowered by the Slough East signalman when the latter signal had been cleared by Slough Middle Signal Box.

Seen from a compartment of the West of England express with men standing and working on the Up main line. Clearly the human psyche at wishing to observe the aftermath of an accident is not a new phenomenon. *Slough Public Library*

The West of England express had been equipped with the automatic vacuum brake in compliance with the Government's Regulation of Railways Act 1889 which legally required all passenger trains operating in the United Kingdom to be fitted with an automatic continuous brake. Yet despite this and the many other improvements to railway safety during the interim, it had still not proved possible to prevent the disaster.

The first task of Lieutenant Colonel H.A. Yorke of the Railway Department of the Board of Trade, who had been appointed to investigate the accident, was to confirm that the signals were at danger behind the Windsor train and secondly to establish why the crew of the express had totally ignored them.

The eastern approach to Slough was controlled by two signal boxes. Slough East Box sited at the eastern end of the station's island platform and Dolphin Signal Box just over a mile away.

Shortly after the passage of the Windsor train Signalman William Charles Colbourn at Dolphin Signal Box had received a request for 'line clear' on the down main line from the signalman at Langley Signal Box. This box was one mile 308 yards away and the next block post towards Paddington. The approaching train was the 1.15pm West of England express which had left Paddington at 1.16pm some four minutes behind the Windsor train. Since the section between Langley and Dolphin Signal Boxes was unobstructed Colbourn gave 'Line Clear.' Two minutes later at 1.37pm, Colbourn offered the express to Slough East Signal Box but because the down main line was still blocked by the Windsor train which had still not left the station, Slough East Box simply acknowledged the bell code. Colbourn then received the bell code for 'Fast Train Approaching' from Langley Signal Box and immediately forwarded this message to Slough East. One minute later at 1.38pm Colbourn received 'Train Entering Section' from Langley and he again asked Slough East if the line was clear.

At 1.40pm Slough East responded with the message 'Section Clear but Junction Blocked.' This meant that Colbourn was required to halt the express at his home signal and verbally instruct the driver to proceed slowly to the Slough East home signal just under a mile away and 227yds. from the rear of the Windsor train. But before Colbourn could finish booking the details of these messages into his train register the express roared past his box at 50 to 60mph overrunning both Dolphin Signal Box's distant and home signals which were still at danger.

Colbourn caught a fleeting glimpse of the fireman leaning over the cab side of the locomotive and immediately sent 'Train Entering Section' to Slough East before grabbing the telephone in an unsuccessful bid to warn his colleagues that the express had ignored his signals and was heading straight towards them.

Whilst the bell code for 'Train Entering Section' had been received by Slough East Box the telephone bell was not heard and consequently it was not until Signalman Cheney spotted the express overrunning his home signal that he realised that anything was wrong.

For some inexplicable reason the express had ignored Dolphin Signal Box's down distant and home signals and had also passed the Slough East down distant signal all of which had been at danger. That afternoon the Paddington milk train had preceded the express by a minute or so at 1.40pm but all the down relief line signals had been returned to danger prior to the arrival of the West of England Express. Signalman Wardall was confident that it was only after the express had passed under the overbridge 595 yards from the rear of the Windsor train and nearly reached the Slough East home signal that steam had been shut off. Adding that by the time the express entered the platform the locomotive had been reversed and steam reapplied.

The express had begun its fateful journey at 1.16pm, one minute late. No.3015 *'Kennet'* one of the GWR's magnificent 7 ft. 8 inch single wheeler locomotives had puffed gracefully out of Paddington station and into the afternoon sunshine, rhythmically accelerating past the unkempt rows of buildings that hemmed the line and before long the great single driving wheels were spinning round with the effortless grace of gyroscopes. Steam was momentarily shut off, as the express passed Hayes sleeper depot; and then with a clear road ahead *'Kennet'* picked up speed and headed towards Reading, the train's first stop.

On the footplate of *'Kennet'* was Driver Henry George Woodman, a driver for 29 years and a first class driver since 1882. He had commenced duty at Bristol at 5.30am that morning with Fireman Cann. Their first duty had been the 6.30am up passenger train from Bristol which arrived at Paddington at 10.32am. The 1.15pm Paddington to West of England express was their final duty for the day and would take them home to Bristol. But before this the locomotive had to be turned and serviced at the nearby Westbourne Locomotive Shed.

Fireman Cann stayed with *'Kennet'* at Westbourne Shed but Driver Woodman left the depot and went to the Great Western Coffee Tavern at nearby Westbourne Park for a meal of ham and coffee.

At 12.55pm with Driver Woodman and Fireman Cann on the footplate *'Kennet'* left the shed and backed onto its train of nine eight-wheeler carriages and one six-wheeler which was standing in Paddington's Platform 3. After the locomotive had been coupled up, Woodman tested the vacuum train brake and found it in perfect order. (The express weighed in total 292 tons excluding passengers.)

After passing the Hayes Sleeper Depot, Driver Woodman notched up the screw reverser and put the regulator just past the central position and steadying himself on the reverser handle leaned out of the cab to watch the road. As an experienced driver he had developed almost a perfect partnership with *'Kennet'* and could immediately respond to even its slightest falter. So much so that he might have bragged to his family and friends that he could drive *'Kennet'* in his sleep.

The approach to Slough was normally uneventful and the express would usually race through under clear signals in a flurry of smoke and steam. Driver Woodman peered into the distance but for some reason he became mesmerised by the track racing towards him. He could remember passing the distant, home and starting signals at Langley Signal Box but then his concentration gradually drifted; well known landmarks, bridges and even signals passed by but made no impression on his mind.

Fireman Cann was busily firing *'Kennet'* keeping the needle of the pressure gauge pressed up against the 160lbs per square inch mark. He broke off to check that the signals at Langley were off and then continued firing. Looking up after his next round with the shovel, Cann thought that the Slough East Distant signal seemed to have been at danger. After confirming this by looking back along the train he then leaned over the cab side and peered through the smoke and steam beating back from the locomotive's chimney only to discover that the home signal which could now be seen for the first time was also at danger. Both signals were sited on the left hand side of the down main line. Yet Driver Woodman had taken no action to brake the express and seemed to be about to overrun the rapidly approaching home signal.

Fireman Cann shouted a desperate 'Whoa!' before leaping across the cab and shutting the regulator and grabbing the brake handle slamming on the brakes. Only then did Driver Woodman come out of his daze and realise his perilous predicament. He went to shut the regulator and apply the brake but on doing so found Fireman Cann's hand

Looking back at the accident from the Up Main platform. This and the view on the next page were clearly taken at a similar time. *Slough Public Library*

had got there first. Woodman spun the reverser into back gear and one or other of them reopened the regulator. Woodman then turned on the steam sand blast valves hoping that the additional grip would stop the wheels from skidding: he could do no more other than brace himself for the inevitable collision with the rear of the train that was blocking his path.

To his credit Driver Woodman readily admitted that whilst he had seen the Slough East Home Signal he had missed both the signals at Dolphin which were sited on his side of the cab between the down and up main lines as well as the Slough East distant signal. He was adamant that he had not been asleep and claimed that if he had been, then, from the position in which he had been standing, he would have fallen off the locomotive.

Driver Woodman had worked the express once every three weeks for fourteen or fifteen years and during that time the line was invariably clear to Reading. He had never been checked by the signals at Dolphin Signal Box. Richard Kelly, the guard of the express, confirmed that the train had been checked at Dolphin Signal Box on previous occasions but it had never been stopped. Fireman Cann added that he had never known the express to be either checked or stopped at Dolphin Signal Box before. But Signalman William Colbourn confirmed that he had personally halted the 1.15pm express at Dolphin as recently as the 2nd and 9th June.

Fireman Cann's prompt action had slowed the express and minimised the force of the impact but, as Inspector Yorke pointed out in his official report, Cann was only doing his job for it was as much his responsibility to look out for signals as Driver Woodman's. It was nevertheless a sobering thought that, but for Fireman Cann's timely action the express would have run into the back of Windsor train at full speed.

Driver Woodman had a good record. (On Thursday 21 April 1881 when driving the early morning goods train he had collided with empty carriages standing in Clevedon

Considering the carnage seen and the number of passengers on the Windsor service, it is perhaps surprising there were only five passenger fatalities although there were 35 who were seriously injured. A small fire also started as a result of timber from the damaged coaches being ignited by heat from the chimney of No 3015, but this was soon extinguished.

Slough Public Library

station pushing them into the street beyond – but no one had been injured.) He was well regarded by his superiors and had no worries. An eye specialist confirmed that his eyesight was good for his age although he needed spectacles for reading. On this basis Lieutenant Colonel Yorke was satisfied that poor vision had not contributed to the accident. Woodman had seen the signals but for some unexplained reason his brain had not responded to them. Lieutenant Colonel Yorke could do nothing more than attribute the cause of the accident to this anomaly.

The Inspector also observed that Woodman, who was nearly sixty years old looked at least ten years older. Since the aging process affected drivers differently, he strongly recommended that all drivers and particularly express train drivers should be medically examined after the age of 55 years. Under the current regulations Woodman would have been examined for the first time in December 1910 when he reached the age of sixty.

Lieutenant Colonel Yorke also observed that, Kelly, the train guard might have averted the tragedy if, instead of concentrating on sorting parcels, he had been looking out for the signals.

Some concern had also been expressed at the doubtful wisdom of running the West of England Express so closely behind the Windsor train. But, as the Inspector explained, the normal interval between the two trains was ten minutes but on the fateful day, owing to the Windsor train being delayed, the gap had been cut to only three or four minutes. This would have been unsatisfactory if the old Time Interval system of signalling had been still in operation but this system had been superseded by Block Signalling under which regulations trains were separated by an interval of space rather than time. As he pointed out when the express had left Paddington, the Windsor train was more than a mile in front. Even so Driver Woodman had been unaware that he was running so closely behind the Windsor train. The late departure of the Windsor train and the extra two-minute delay at Slough had been crucial elements in the disaster.

Lieutenant Colonel Yorke acknowledged that the facilities at Slough were insufficient for the level of traffic handled on race days and also criticised the Company's use of the 'calling on' arrangements. The practice had been previously highlighted as unsafe by the Board of Trade following two serious accidents and the Associated Railway Companies had been requested to ask its members to reduce the use of the arrangement to the absolute minimum. At Slough the arrangement should have been restricted solely to trains required to stop at Slough and certainly not used in relation to fast through trains such as the West of England Express. The GWR subsequently omitted the Slough stop and ran the 1.05pm train from Paddington straight through to Windsor.

'Train Braking and Stopping Distances.'

Driver Woodman had been at fault for the disaster but a more thorough investigation into the accident could have revealed that he was a victim of circumstances largely out of his control. The type of locomotive involved, the train's braking arrangements and the GWR's version of the vacuum brake all had a bearing on the accident.

Unlike his earlier Victorian forbears at the Railway Department of the Board of Trade, Yorke had not investigated the poor braking performance of the Express or tested the stopping distance of a similarly loaded train braking from the same speed in as near as possible identical conditions. Questions concerning train braking distances had been asked at the inquests but this important aspect was omitted from the official report.

At the Paddington Inquest T.I. Allen the Chief Superintendent of the GWR had observed that a train travelling at 50mph would need 400 to 500yds. or between 1,200 and 1,500 feet to pull up. At the same Inquest Richard Kelly, the guard of the express, stated that the vacuum brake should have stopped the express in 400 yards and if it had been applied at the Slough East Distant Signal then the express could have been easily pulled up before the station.

The West of England Express had been travelling at between 50 – 60 mph on the almost straight and perfectly level approach to Slough in dry and sunny conditions. Fireman Cann stated in his evidence that the regulator was shut and the brake applied between the distant and home signals for Slough East which were sited 1,175 yds. and 227 yds. respectively from the point of impact. The brake was hard on by the home signal and by this time driver Woodman had or was in the process of reversing *'Kennet'*. Richard Kelly who was riding in his van, the seventh vehicle from the locomotive, confirmed that a full application of the vacuum train brake had been made between the over bridge 594 yds. away from the rear of the Windsor train and the home signal. Yet at Slough signal box only a matter of 31 yds. from the rear of the Windsor train the speed of the express had only been reduced to 20-25 mph. If the brake had been applied by the over bridge as the evidence seemed to suggest then it was reasonable to have expected the express to have been safely halted before reaching the rear of the Windsor train.

The Times newspaper had reported the tragic events at Slough and the proceedings of the three separate inquests at Windsor, Slough, and Paddington into the deaths of the three passengers who had been killed outright and two others who had succumbed to their injuries. It had also reported the Assize Hearing at Reading at which Driver Woodman had been found not guilty of the manslaughter charge (brought by the Windsor Coroner's Jury) and discharged.

The Times also reported two letters from members of the public. The first of these called for the addition of a third crew member in the cab of each locomotive specifically to look out for signals. Modern locomotives, the writer claimed, required closer attention; train lengths and weights had increased, and with the added responsibility of steam brakes and the communication cord he reasoned that footplate duties were now too onerous for two men to carry out in safety.

Following the publication of Lieutenant Colonel H.A. Yorke's Official Report on the accident in early November 1900, a second and far more credible letter was published by the Times on 30 November 1900. The writer, who used the pseudonym 'Engineer,' described himself as an experienced well travelled engineer who was qualified to compare United Kingdom railway practice with that in the remainder of the world. Rather like an independent witness or expert consultant, he had reviewed Lieutenant Colonel Yorke's report and by appraising the evidence was able to provide an important conclusion totally missing from the Official Report.

On foreign railways, the 'Engineer' claimed, train brakes were far more effective in stopping trains than here in Britain. Had a situation similar to that at Slough occurred elsewhere in the world he was sure that the express could have been stopped and a disaster averted. He exonerated Britain's railways for this situation since they were only complying with the braking methods approved by the Board of Trade some twenty years earlier. Having carefully analysed the witness statements of both the driver and fireman of the West of England Express set out in the Official Report, (these were reproduced in his letter to the Times), he had determined that the express's brakes had been applied immediately prior to the overbridge 594yds. from the point of collision, at which point the express had been travelling at a speed of 50 or 60 mph. The track was level and presumably in good condition. Yet as the witness testimonies clearly indicated, the express ran at least 1,782 feet after the train brakes had been applied and with the locomotive reversed for nearly half that distance. Despite this at the end of 1,782 feet the train's speed, moments before the collision, was still 25 to 30 mph.

The writer pointed out that in other countries, to compensate for the sometimes less sophisticated signalling systems, greater reliance had to be placed on train braking to maintain safety. This had led to the development of highly efficient train braking systems. Using a formula derived from the practical experience of these systems, it was possible to determine in what distance a train travelling at a certain speed could be stopped without slipping the wheels given a level track in good condition. The formula stated:- 'distance in feet required to stop was equal to one third of the square of the speed in miles per hour'.

The formula applied to level track but it had been established by experimentation that only in cases of bad rail or inefficient brakes should the stipulated distances be exceeded by more than 50%. It was the writer's view that in moderate practice it should only be appropriate to exceed the stipulated distances by 25% unless the rail was slippery.

Using this formula and allowing an additional margin of 25%, he had calculated that a train travelling at 50mph could be stopped in 1,041 feet, 55mph – 1,260 feet and 60 mph – 1,500 feet. He observed that these braking distances were achieved on a daily basis, without reversing the locomotive and that a train could be brought to a full stop within that distance. He ended his letter by pointing out that in the United Kingdom the middle wheel set of six wheeled carriages and locomotive bogie wheels were normally unbraked.

The mystery expert made it abundantly clear that the express should have completely stopped within 1,500 feet and certainly should not have exceeded this distance by 282 feet or worse still be travelling at a speed of 25 – 30 mph. Damning evidence indeed! (A table of braking distances set out in a locomotive text book published in the United Kingdom in 1908 used the same formula but added an additional 75% to the overall braking distance. The author of this book observed that the distances could be halved with improvements to locomotive braking, braking design and rapidity of application.)

'Complacency and an Intrinsic Defect.'

The 'Engineer' might not have had access to the axle loadings of the various classes of GWR locomotives. Had this been readily available he might have made even more damaging observations.

The first major difference between British and world wide railway operation was that in Britain the majority of companies had adopted the simpler automatic vacuum train brake system. Although used on several railways in the United Kingdom, the rival Westinghouse air braking system had been widely adopted elsewhere, particularly in Europe and North America. The Westinghouse system provided an automatic continuous brake and thereby met the requirements of the Board of Trade, but was more complicated despite, arguably, being the more efficient train brake.

The second major difference between British and worldwide railway operation was in locomotive policy. Apart from one or two instances overseas, railways had long abandoned the single wheeler type of locomotive in favour of the larger coupled wheeled types which now held almost universal sway. In Britain during the 1880s the single wheeler locomotive had undergone a revival with the advent of steam sanding equipment and such locomotives had turned in some remarkable performances. The GWR with its flat and level main line had always stayed loyal to this type of locomotive and had used them on its principal trains from the very outset with the type remaining in daily use until the end of the broad gauge in 1892. Indeed when replacement narrow gauge locomotives were needed for the express services between Paddington and the West of England it was inevitable that the traditionalist GWR would construct locomotives of the single wheeler type.

The 'Achilles' Class or '3031' Class, designed by William Dean, had been originally built as 2-2-2 tender locomotives but a derailment in Box Tunnel on 16 September 1893 attributable to excess weight at the front end caused them to be rebuilt to the 4-2-2 configuration. No.3015 *'Kennet'* had been built at Swindon in April 1892 and rebuilt as a 4-2-2 in August 1894. The class comprised a total of eighty locomotives with the last twenty being built at Swindon Works as recently as 1897 and 1899.

These locomotives, with their impressive 7 feet 8 inch driving wheels, when given a suitable load and level line could turn in stunning performances. Indeed, on 4 May 1904 almost four years after the Slough collision, fellow 'Achilles' Class member No.3065 *'Duke of Connaught'* which had replaced record breaking 'City Class' 4-4-0 *'City of Truro'* at Bristol, had not only taken the American Mails to Paddington at an average speed of 71.5 mph but had maintained an average speed of 80 mph for a distance of 73 miles!

Although the single wheeler type of locomotive had the advantages of free running and economy it had an insuperable disadvantage compared to the larger 4-4-0 or 4-6-0 types of locomotive. This was apparent as trains became longer and heavier and meant that the 4-2-2 type became not only deficient in terms of adhesion but more importantly in braking power. The old adage about the art of train driving not being in getting the train to move but in stopping was particularly applicable to this type of locomotive.

On *'Kennet'*, in common with other locomotives of the 4-2-2 configuration, only the driving, trailing and tender wheels were braked. The heavy leading bogie which carried a weight of 18 tons was unbraked. Adding the weight carried by the driving wheel (18 tons) together with that carried by the braked trailing wheel (13 tons) the braked weight of *'Kennet'* as a % of its total weight of 49 tons was 63.3% (or if the trailing wheel is excluded from the calculation 36.7%) (the tender weight being excluded from both this and the following calculations).

By comparison a 'Badminton Class' (old '3292 Class') 4-4-0 again with an unbraked bogie but with coupled wheels had a total braked weight of (17 Tons 1 cwt + 15 Tons 6 cwt) or 61.5% expressed as a percentage of its total weight of 52 tons 3 cwt. Slightly less than the 63.3% of the 'Achilles' Class.

In contrast the 'Dean Goods' 0-6-0 tender locomotives with all driving wheels braked (15 tons + 15 tons + 13 tons 5 cwt) meant that its total weight of 43 tons 5 cwt was also 100% of its braked weight.

As well as having a much reduced percentage of braked weight available *'Kennet'* was also seriously disadvantaged by the type of brake fitted. In common with current GWR practice the Class was not equipped with the vacuum brake but with a combination steam brake vacuum brake system.

From an examination of photographs it appears that the 'Achilles Class' was equipped with two separate steam brake cylinders located under the left and right hand side of the cab. These, by the use of a combined linkage, applied single brake blocks to the leading wheel tyres of the 7 feet 8 inch driving and 4 feet 7 inch diameter trailing wheels. Because of the greater inherent kinetic energy and the reciprocating weight of the motion attached to the massive 7 feet 8 inch driving wheel, this would take longer to stop than the smaller trailing wheel and it is probable that this factor had to be accommodated in the design of the brake linkage principally to ensure that the trailing wheel did not lock up and skid under heavy braking. The problem was that if this occurred its contribution to the overall retardation of the locomotive would be totally lost. To avoid this, the brake linkage for the trailing wheel set would need to ensure that the brake was applied with marginally less force than that applied to the single driving wheel. Therefore the time taken to retard the large driving wheel from a given speed without skidding would determine the braking distance for the locomotive with the trailing wheel only exerting a subsidiary braking effect. The same problem of minimising wheel locking would also need to be addressed with the steam braking arrangements for the tender wheels.

If this hypothesis is correct then from the point of view of the locomotive's braking arrangements adopted for this type of locomotive there was a serious design weakness which would give rise to excessive braking distances when compared to that achievable by other types of locomotives with different wheel arrangements. Even the contemporary 'Badminton' Class 4-4-0 which although having a similar % braked weight to the 'Achilles' Class did not have the same inherent defect since its rear driving wheel was not only connected to the leading driving wheel but was also identical in diameter. So in practice neither could lock up independently of the other and the 'Badminton' Class would theoretically be capable of out-braking an 'Achilles' Class locomotive.

Indeed there is no reference in the report to any of the wheel tyres of the locomotive or tender being found to have flat spots which would infer that the wheels had not locked up under braking and had still been revolving immediately prior to the collision.

A further shortcoming was the use of steam instead of vacuum to operate the locomotive's brakes. The carriages of the express were equipped with the vacuum train brake which was applied by the admission of air to the train pipe when either the driver or guard opened the valve under their direct control. But this action also automatically opened a steam valve which proportionately applied the steam brake to the locomotive and tender. The most important drawback of the steam brake was that when a full brake application was made at high speed it did not respond as quickly as the vacuum brake particularly when cold. A second application made once the cylinders were warm had greater effect but in an emergency a second attempt might not always be possible. This was an additional deficiency which would undermined the braking ability of the 'Achilles Class' even further.

'Questions in Parliament.'

A Bristol newspaper alleged that immediately after the collision driver Woodman had stated that his brakes had failed; although this admission was later retracted. But when Woodman was committed to trial upon the charge of manslaughter sureties of £10 each were given by no less a personages than Mr Waister, Assistant Locomotive Superintendent and Mr John Armstrong, District Locomotive Superintendent of the GWR. Perhaps Woodman's superiors recognised that his initial error had been exacerbated by the inherently indifferent braking characteristics of his locomotive. The applause from fellow railwaymen that greeted his discharge at Reading Assize, suggests that other drivers were sympathetic to his predicament. It should be added that the jury accepted Woodman's explanation for his error and no evidence in relation to the braking of the express was submitted.

The Railway Trade Unions had no faith in the Board of Trade Inspectors, regarding them as little more than Government stooges. On 13 December 1900 the Times reported a statement made on behalf of the Executive Committee, of the Amalgamated Society of Railway Servants by its General Secretary, Mr Richard Bell MP. This took exception to Lieutenant Colonel Yorke's reference to the duties of passenger train guards and their responsibilities for the safe working of trains. Guards were expected to perform a variety of duties which meant it was impossible for them to be alert to every signal. Indeed on some railways the construction of vans made it was impossible to look out for signals from the inside. In relation to Lieutenant Colonel Yorke's Report concerning the driver the Committee went on to say:- 'We are strongly of opinion that if a practical railwayman had investigated the case no such recommendations would have been made, for we are convinced that they are useless.'

No less than three Members of Parliament had been travelling on the Windsor train and a further Member of Parliament had been a passenger on the West of England Express and it is therefore not surprising that the issue of train braking was raised in the House of Commons on 13 December 1900. Mr Kearley, MP for Devonport, asked the President of the Board of Trade the following questions:- whether his expert advisers believed the Slough accident might have been avoided if the train had been fitted with the most modern high speed brakes; whether from the moment the brakes were applied until the collision occurred the distance covered was about 600 yds. and the speed was diminished from 55 to 20mph; and whether he was aware that in other countries trains running at a similar speed could be brought to a standstill in less than 350yds. He concluded by asking whether under the circumstances the President of the Board of Trade proposed to take any steps to inquire into the efficiency of brakes on all English railways?

The President of the Board of Trade Mr Gerald Balfour MP for Leeds Central, replied that the Inspecting Officer was of the opinion that the disaster could not have been entirely avoided even if the train had been fitted with 'modern high speed brakes.' The evidence was unclear at which point the brakes had been applied since the men who had not been watching the signals would not be exact as to where the train was when the brakes were applied. The Inspecting Officer's personal opinion was that the moment of application was little more than 200yds. from the point of collision. (This discounted the evidence of both Fireman Cann and Guard Kelly who were sure that the train brake had been applied well before the Slough East Home Signal 227 yards from the point of collision). Whilst it was agreed that train brakes in this Country could be made equally effective over a similar distance, the Board of Trade was unable to press railway companies to adopt a particular brake but could only hope that they would take advantage of any improvements.

The President also referred to a letter from the General Manager of the GWR advising that:- 'The directors have already ordered that a new and exhaustive series of experiments as to the efficiency of the brake power upon their trains shall be arranged in the coming spring.'

'A Thorough Reappraisal of Train Braking.'

In the light of these experiments G.J. Churchward, who had replaced William Dean as GWR Locomotive Superintendent in June 1902, decreed that in future all large express locomotives should be equipped with the vacuum brake (which would provide instantaneous braking) instead of the steam brake and that the leading bogies of all 4-6-0 type locomotives should be fitted with brakes ensuring that the highest proportion of a locomotive's weight was braked. (Later experimentation proved that the bogie brakes added little to a locomotive's braking power and being difficult to maintain were subsequently removed.) The percentage of braked weight for a 'Saint Class' 4-6-0 locomotive was a very respectable 75% of its total weight of 72 tons (18 tons + 18 tons + 18 tons) or 100% if the 17 ton weight of the leading bogie was included.

Comparative tests undertaken as part of the experiments referred to in the General Manager's letter to the President of the Board of Trade also resulted in major changes to the vacuum brake. The GWR had been proud that its own version of the vacuum brake which utilised sliding brake cylinders was superior to rival designs but in 1903 these too were replaced by more efficient brake cylinders mounted on trunions.

The accident had also highlighted a fundamental deficiency in the design of the vacuum brake notably in relation to applications made at high train speed. For the vacuum brake to operate, air had to be admitted to the train pipe which ran the full length of the train connecting the various vacuum brake cylinders of each individual vehicle. Air could only gain access to the train pipe from the point of application and therefore the time required for the air to pass into the pipe to destroy the vacuum took valuable seconds delaying the effective application of the brake. This would particularly affect the rearmost vehicles of a long train when for example the driver initiated the vacuum brake application.

This time delay was reduced by incorporating Direct Admission (DA) valves into the vacuum brake system which automatically admitted air to the train's vacuum brake cylinders whenever a full brake or emergency application was made. But the valves were designed in such a way as to still allow the driver to exert a degree of control over the amount of brake application. With this modification the effectiveness of the vacuum brake was drastically improved and the delay encountered when braking in an emergency at a high speed largely minimised.

The 'Achilles Class' 4-2-2 locomotives, despite their free running, economies of operation and the benefit of steam sanding equipment, were simply unable to keep pace with the increasing rise in train weights prior to the First World War. These had increased to such an extent that many of the 4-4-0 classes were unable to cope. *'Kennet'* was withdrawn in June 1908 and the remainder of the class of 80 locomotives had been scrapped by the end of 1915. It was an ignominious end for perhaps one of the most handsome classes of locomotives ever built by the GWR.

'An Absolutely Failsafe Device – The Birth of ATC.'

In an age of rapid mechanical and scientific progress, the press found it ironic that no one had invented a mechanical device to prevent train drivers passing signals at danger. Human error had triggered the collision at Slough and it was recognised that this and similar accidents could only be prevented by removing the human factor which so far had always seemed able to successfully circumvent any advance in train safety. Lieutenant Colonel Yorke's report had devoted several paragraphs highlighting the urgent need for such a device but adding that unless this could be made totally foolproof its use would pose an even greater danger by introducing a further potential hazard. The failure of such a device might instead of preventing an accident cause one since a driver might over rely on the device and ignore the external warning signals. Several promising devices had been developed but making them absolutely failsafe had always proved to be an insuperable stumbling block.

It was to be to the everlasting credit of the GWR that it overcame these difficulties and developed a failsafe mechanical device which ensured train safety by giving the driver an audible warning of whether the home signal ahead was at danger or clear. With further development the system finally achieved the ultimate goal of preventing drivers ignoring danger signals.

In January 1906 prototype audible distant signals were installed on the GWR's Henley Branch. The apparatus which was sited a quarter of a mile away from a distant signal – (except where the signal was the lower arm of a stop signal, in which case, it was placed at the signal,) - comprised a ramped insulated steel bar about 44 ft. long attached to a length of timber laid centrally between the rails. When a locomotive equipped with the necessary spring contact shoe passed over the ramp, the shoe which was attached to the underside of the locomotive, was raised a distance of 1 ½ inches. When the distant signal was 'all right' the ramp was electrified. In this instance the current ran through the shoe holding up an armature in the locomotive's cab which in turn energised a relay that rang a bell. In normal running this armature was kept closed by a current from a battery on the locomotive. The ramp was sufficiently long to enable the driver to receive the audible signal that the section ahead was clear, at the very highest speeds, and the bell was sufficiently loud to enable the signal to be heard above all other engine noises. Should the signal be at 'caution' then the ramp remained electrically dead (as it would if the electrical circuit between it and the signal box had failed). The action of raising the shoe broke the electrical circuit on the locomotive causing the armature in apparatus carried by the locomotive to drop, sounding a steam whistle in the cab which remained in operation until switched off by the driver.

The system proved to be so successful that a further trial was undertaken on the Company's Fairford and Lambourn branches. Then in November 1908 the system was installed at all the distant signals between Reading and Slough and two years later extended to Paddington. By the expedient of linking the system to the locomotive's vacuum brake it evolved into a reliable method of automatic train control which not only gave an audible signal to the driver but if for any reason the driver failed to cancel or respond to the warning, the leakage of air into the braking system, which now sounded a warning siren, (in place of the steam whistle) would bring the train to a stand without the intervention of the fireman.

Automatic Train Control quickly became the driver's best friend whatever the weather conditions. But even so drivers were not encouraged to regard the apparatus as a substitute for keeping watch on the road ahead.

In 1929 the system was extended to the remainder of the Great Western's main as well as some secondary routes. By 1939 most of the Companies network had been equipped and over 3,000 locomotives, diesel railcars and auto cars fitted with the necessary apparatus.

Automatic Train Control was the GWR's guardian angel for it meant that unlike other companies, trains could be run in perfect safety in falling snow or dense fogs even if the signals could be not be seen. Commenting on its use in November 1946 a driver explained: 'I will say that it is appreciated very much by the staff especially in the conditions we shall be having after all this rain. I should be lost without the ATC. I know I should not say it, but that is a fact, and the ATC takes us from one end of the GWR to the other.'

Lieutenant Colonel Yorke's successors at the Railway Department repeatedly called upon other railway companies to install ATC but to no avail. It was not until 1958 that British Railways began work on installing its own version of ATC, the Automatic Warning System (AWS).

At the Great Western Railway Company's Half Yearly meeting in August 1900 a disgruntled shareholder contrasted his decreasing dividend with the magnificent carriages and other extravagances and suggested that the Company was managed like a philanthropic society. In some ways it was; the Directors had a patriarchal regard for their passengers well being and were also acutely aware of the public's perception of the Company. The Slough disaster had rammed home the dangers of complacency when it came to train safety. The Company responded to the challenge by using some of its massive revenues to ensure that to the best of its abilities such a tragedy could never happen again. In making the GWR one of the safest railways in Britain there can be little doubt that this was down to Automatic Train Control and with hindsight this was the GWR's greatest triumph of all.

The tender of 'Kennet' may be seen with the roof and end of a damaged vehicle from the Windsor service on the 'Up Main'. Clearly news of the accident had travelled fast for a local photographer to be summoned to take the images accompanying this piece. *Slough Public Library*

A final view from Slough, this time with clearance work in progress as witness the presence of the crane on the extreme left. No 3015 was repaired and continued in service until June 1908. The damage to the station footbridge and canopy will also be seen from the various views. It was also fortunate that there was no fire caused by escaping gas from the carriage lighting system. 65 rail chairs and 36 sleepers were also broken or destroyed whilst there was some damage to office doors in the station building, caused no doubt by flying debris,

Formation (rear to front) of the 1.05 ex Paddington as listed in Lieutenant Colonel H. A. Yorke's report:			
No. 3390	Brake-Third	8-wheel	Completely smashed
No. 657	Tri-composite	8-wheel	Completely smashed
No. 745	Composite	8-wheel	End compartment smashed and other damage
No. 855	Composite	8-wheel	One compartment at either end smashed and other damage
No. 3047	Third-class	8-wheel	Damage to quarter lights and buffers
No. 1926	Third-class	8-wheel	Damage to buffing gear
No. 983	Brake-composite	8-wheel	Damage to buffing gear
No. 2904	Brake–third	8-wheel	Damage to buffing gear
Note - Photographic evidence shows that No 855 was the third carriage from the rear, not No 745.			
Formation (front to rear) of the 1.15 pm ex Paddington (damaged vehicles only):			
No. 2053	Brake-third	8-wheel	Minor damage to body and buffing gear
No. 1410	Composite	8-wheel	Minor damage to body and buffing gear
No. 947	Composite	8-wheel	Minor damage to body and buffing gear
No. 2054	Brake-third	8-wheel	Damage to body and buffing gear
No 1699	Third-class	6-wheel	Minor damage

'Man of the Great Western'

ALLAN STEPHEN QUARTERMAINE

Mention the name Allan Quartermaine to most of the present generation and it is likely one of two images will emerge: the protagonist from H Rider Haggard's 1885 novel 'King Solomon's Mines', or more recently as a closely resembled character in the fourth of the 'Indiana Jones' quartet of films.

So far as railways and in particular the GWR were concerned, the name Allan Quartermaine should instead refer to the last Chief Engineer of the 'old company', who continued on as the first Chief Civil Engineer for the Western Region of British Railways.

Born on 9 November 1888, Mr Quartermaine had first joined the GWR in 1910 based in the Divisional Engineer's Office at Wolverhampton. Three years later he moved to the Chief Engineer's Office at Paddington before seeing military service with the Royal Engineers constructing railways in Egypt and Palestine. In connection with his military work he was mentioned in despatches and also awarded the Military Cross. Returning to the GWR in 1920, he was appointed assistant to the divisional engineer at Gloucester, returning again to Paddington in 1924, this time as assistant to the joint chief engineers. At the same time he was promoted to the rank of Major in the Regular Army Reserve of Officers.

Further promotion followed, Divisional Engineer Bristol in January 1926 and then in 1929 as assistant chief engineer (permanent way and docks) in 1933.

Appointed the GWR Chief Engineer in January 1940, WW2 also saw him acting as Director-General of Aircraft production factories under Lord Beaverbrook. For his wartime work he was awarded a CBE in 1943.

His retired from the BR Western Region in 1951, being elected president of the Institute of Civil Engineers for the session 1951-52. After his railway career he was appointed a member of the Royal Fine Art Commission and was also knighted in 1956. He retired from the RFAC in 1960 and continued to live in retirement until his death on 17 October 1978 just 23 days before what would have been his 90th birthday.

A Photographic 'POTPOURRI'

Opposite page *- One of a small batch of Engineer's Inspection Saloons built around the end of the 19th century for use around the system. -* *see also p89.* *Dependent upon need, the vehicle might be attached to a normal train or more usually form a special working being hauled or propelled as required, and if the latter a warning bell similar to that on the front of an auto -trailer was provided. (Russell 'Appendix Vol 2' Fig 564 shows one of this type of vehicle with a seat attached to the end buffer beam.) One vehicle was attached to each division and might be used by the permanent way engineer or other senior official. All appear to have been out of use by early BR days with the lower view showing one seemingly dumped and out of use at Fenny Compton. The location of the coach in the top view is not recorded.*

Above *- 'Bulldog' 4-4-0 'Evan Llewellyn' at Reading shed on 13 April 1927 and with the addition of a robin's nest on top of the rear offside spring of the tender. Whether the robin had been a fast worker, or the engine had been out of service for a time allowing the nest to be built is not reported.*

Puzzle and amusement to conclude the final page. The ***top*** *view clearly shows a steam-railmotor but it is NOT the wonderful 21st century reincarnation by the Great Western Society. So, where and why would a railmotor have been bedecked as seen? Clearly an opening or celebration of sorts as witness the flags, but when, where and why....?*

Left *- Hide and seek perhaps on a camping coach holiday, again no location. Now there is an idea for camping coach holidays that surely could be revived by our various heritage lines..... .*

We hope you have enjoyed our dip into the archives and history of the Great Western Railway.

There could well be more......so if this type of coverage appeals, please make sure the publisher / editor is informed.

INDEX

Figures in bold refer to illustrations or information within captions.

INDEX